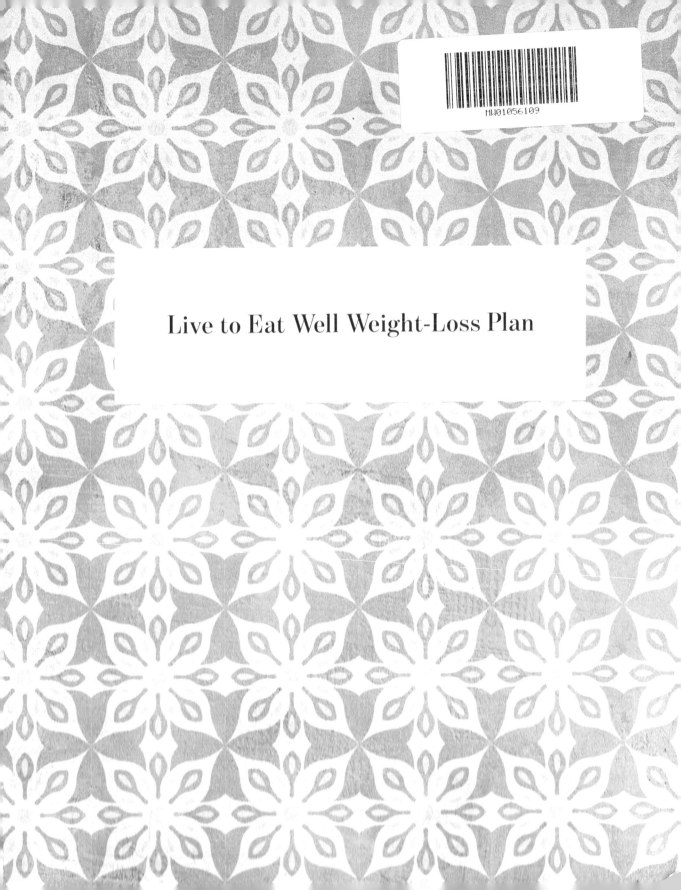

Live to Eat Well Weight-Loss Plan

live to eat well

Weight-Loss Plan

100 Mediterranean Diet Recipes for Healthy Living

SARAH PFLUGRADT, MS, RDN, CSCS

PHOTOGRAPHY BY ANDREW PURCELL

ROCKRIDGE
PRESS

For general information on our other products and services or to obtain technical support, please contact our Customer Care Department within the United States at (866) 744-2665, or outside the United States at (510) 253-0500.

Rockridge Press publishes its books in a variety of electronic and print formats. Some content that appears in print may not be available in electronic books, and vice versa.

TRADEMARKS: Rockridge Press and the Rockridge Press logo are trademarks or registered trademarks of Callisto Media Inc. and/or its affiliates, in the United States and other countries, and may not be used without written permission. All other trademarks are the property of their respective owners. Rockridge Press is not associated with any product or vendor mentioned in this book.

Interior and Cover Designer: Richard Tapp
Art Producer: Samantha Ulban
Editor: Adrian Potts
Production Editor: Matt Burnett
Production Manager: Holly Haydash

Photography © 2021 Andrew Purcell, Food Styling by Carrie Purcell. Illustrations © Charlie Layton, pp. 29-34.
Author photograph courtesy of Kellyn Wilson Photography.

Cover: Chicken Gyro Bowl, page 150

ISBN: Print 978-1-64739-671-8 | eBook 978-1-64739-395-3

R0

To Henry, Lily, Eva, and Luke, the four best taste testers in the world, who are far more adventurous eaters than I will ever be and who will always try anything once. To my dad, from our Missouri-to-California road trip with no cell phone 22 years ago, to video chatting across the world today, thank you for always supporting me.

SPAGHETTI AGLIO E OLIO WITH SHRIMP, PAGE 139

Contents

Introduction

Congratulations on taking the first step to finding an enjoyable and sustainable way to nourish your body, take control of your weight, and maintain lifelong health.

You are certainly not alone in your desire to lose weight. I am a registered dietitian, but that doesn't mean I have magical powers to keep the scale in check. After struggling with weight in high school and college, I managed to turn things around in my early 20s by embracing exercise, studying nutrition, and developing a love of cooking.

Still, I have the same temptations with food and challenges of balancing work, family, and life as everybody else does. After gaining 40 pounds with my last child, I knew that diet and exercise were my two keys to losing the weight. I gave myself time and grace and fueled my body properly—following the same tenets that underscore the diet in this book—and began to see the results.

Through my work I have helped my clients revamp their diet and lose weight by following Mediterranean-style eating patterns. In this book, I will teach you the same principles to improve your health and live your best life. Perhaps you have a medical condition, such as heart disease, where losing weight can help you reduce your blood pressure and cholesterol levels. Maybe you just had a baby and can't wait to fit back into your favorite jeans. Perhaps you just want to feel more energized. Whatever the reason, it's your reason, and I will show you how nutrition and exercise can get you to where you want to be.

Living in Europe, I have been fortunate to spend time in the Mediterranean region, especially in the south of Italy and Spain. In a part of the world where delicious and wholesome food is an integral part of everyday life, it's no coincidence that these countries have some of the highest life expectancies in the world.

This Mediterranean diet is special. It throws some conventional diet advice out the window, but it also validates what health experts have been saying for years: Eat a plant-forward diet with minimal processed foods and stay active. With the guidance and recipes in this book, you will not only live to eat well by enjoying foods from across the region but also eat to live long by reaping the benefits of a diet that promotes lifelong good health.

Your journey to losing weight and living well the Mediterranean way starts now.

ORANGE AND HONEY POLENTA BARS, PAGE 181

Lose Weight the Mediterranean Way

CHAPTER 1

The Mediterranean Diet and Lifestyle

The cultures of the Mediterranean region vary, but they are bound by a common enjoyment of nourishing food that is woven into the daily fabric of family and social life. As a registered dietitian, I have long been an advocate of the Mediterranean diet for weight control, well-being, and longevity. But what exactly do we mean when we refer to the Mediterranean diet?

Inspired by the countries that border the Mediterranean Sea, the diet combines an active lifestyle with cuisine that emphasizes vegetables, fruits, whole grains, legumes, nuts, olive oil, and some seafood, poultry, and dairy.

This book draws from the best of Mediterranean cooking, using familiar ingredients that are available at your local grocery store. The recipes show you that it's possible to achieve your health goals by enjoying, rather than depriving yourself of, food. The recipes are matched with a 21-day plan in which I share a holistic approach to weight loss that combines exercise and self-care with plenty of tips and tricks to keep you on the path to good eating for the rest of your life.

Downsides of the Standard American Diet

The standard American diet, sometimes referred to as the Western diet, is far from optimal for good health. Juggling the demands of family, work, and commuting, many of us have come to rely on the convenience of take-out meals or highly processed packaged foods. Our preferred way of eating typically includes large amounts of processed red meat, added sugars, and refined grains. As a dietitian, I always say there are no "bad" foods, but there are some that you should limit—and those I just mentioned are high on my list.

It's not just that we often consume a surplus of calories, which are stored in the body as fat. By eating foods high in sugar and sodium, we fail to get the vitamins, minerals, and antioxidants needed to maintain good health. In addition, diets high in saturated fats and simple sugars, and low in omega-3 fatty acids and fiber, have been shown to increase inflammation in the body. Along with obesity, inflammation is at the core of many health problems, including heart disease, type 2 diabetes, and metabolic syndrome, which encompass a cluster of conditions including high blood sugar, high blood pressure, and high cholesterol.

You might think that taking a variety of dietary supplements could alleviate any nutritional deficiencies, but science has not yet been able to bottle up all of the natural goodness in plant-based foods. When these foods are lacking in your diet, so are important nutrients called phytochemicals, which help protect your cells. Different phytonutrients have different jobs; we refer to some as antioxidants, which have been known to reduce inflammation and improve health.

How the Mediterranean Diet Can Help You Lose Weight

So why exactly is the Mediterranean diet so well suited for weight loss? As the meal plan and recipes in this book will show, this diet allows you to eat a full plate of delicious ingredients recommended for good health without exceeding your daily calorie goals. Combined with a lifestyle promotes staying active and keeping stress levels down, you have all the necessary components for a successful weight-loss journey.

A 2018 study published in the journal *Healthcare* found that diets higher in vegetables and lower in sweets were key to the success of weight-loss plans. In addition, they found that a Mediterranean diet helped individuals lose and keep off more weight than a low-fat or low-carb diet.

The Mediterranean Diet Pyramid

As illustrated in the pyramid, fresh fruits and vegetables, grains such as whole-wheat bread, pasta, or rice, and olive oil are important parts of every meal. Foods enjoyed daily include nuts, cheese, or yogurt, and red wine. Fish, eggs, poultry, and legumes are consumed several times a week, and meat is restricted to a few times a month.

Fruits · Vegetables · Whole Grains
Bread · Pasta · Rice · Olive Oil

EVERY MAIN MEAL

Cheese · Yogurt · Nuts · Wine

DAILY

Fish · Eggs · Poultry · Legumes

WEEKLY

Meat

MONTHLY

The 21-Day Plan

This 21-day plan is designed to get you started on developing a lifestyle of healthy eating, helping you lose weight and keep it off for good. You have meals with easy recipes from the book and shopping lists to make it easier to prepare and plan for the diet. Many ingredients are used multiple times in the book, so you won't find yourself buying something that you can't use again. This plan includes grab-and-go recipes, make-ahead tips, cooking tips, easy ingredient substitutions, and ideas for leftovers, so it will be easy for you to stick to it.

This plan offers a holistic approach to your health and for sustained weight loss, including these fundamental pillars:

- Nutrition
- Exercise
- Relaxation
- Sleep

Each of these pillars will be an active part of your 21-day plan, and you'll learn more about each in the chapters to come.

Live to Eat Well

Life is meant to be lived, and lived well. The Mediterranean way of eating encourages you to not only slow down and savor mealtime but also do so without feeling guilty about what you eat.

As Americans, we tend to eat quickly and on the go. We eat in our cars and at our desks, and rush through dinner to get to the next event (or migrate to the sofa). Mediterranean eating is about not only enjoying your food, but also the company you keep. Meals are slower, shared, and purposeful. They nourish not only the body but also the mind and soul.

You won't always be able to take the leisurely route with food, but this 21-day plan will set you up for success so you can begin to see food not as a last-minute, must-do chore, but rather as something you can always enjoy, at home or on the go.

The Mediterranean diet is the opposite of the crash or fad diet, which involves eliminating entire food groups or simply going hungry. You will find that eating a Mediterranean diet gives you the opportunity to enjoy all the foods you love. This "whole diet" approach has been shown to produce more favorable health outcomes than diets that restrict a single nutrient or food group.

Eat to Live Long

Weight loss may be at the top of your list of reasons for trying this diet, but the long-term benefits should keep you eating a Mediterranean-style diet long after you shed the pounds. Good health equals living well—and also living longer. The Mediterranean diet has been studied extensively for its health benefits.

The diet was first recognized in the United States during the 1960s, after a researcher named Ancel Keys observed that the working-class communities in the countries surrounding the Mediterranean Sea had much less heart disease than people in the United States and other northern European countries. Their high intake of vegetables, olive oil, and whole grains, and low intake of red meat and sweets, made him think that this way of eating was beneficial for health. He was right. And while the diet can be adapted to foods we can buy in the United States, the dietary pattern that is recognized to provide health benefits has stayed relatively consistent for 60 years.

THE PHYSICAL HEALTH BENEFITS

Diet-related chronic disease is one of the biggest health problems facing the United States, where life expectancy has actually fallen in recent years. The reverse is true in countries like Italy, Spain, and Israel, where healthy eating and less sedentary lifestyles contribute to residents continuing to live longer on average than nearly anywhere else on the planet.

A 2019 review study published in the *International Journal of Environmental Research and Public Health* summarized the many health benefits of long-term adherence to the Mediterranean lifestyle. They include:

- Reductions in total weight and body fat
- Prevention of heart disease
- Reduced risk of type 2 diabetes
- Prevention of metabolic syndrome

Early research even shows the Mediterranean diet's promise in preventing cognitive disorders such as Alzheimer's and Parkinson's disease, as well as lowering the risk of developing cancer.

HEALTHIER ALSO MEANS HAPPIER

It's not just physical health the Mediterranean diet can benefit. A 2013 study published in the *Journal of Nutrition, Health, and Aging* found that older adults who ate a Mediterranean diet had a decreased risk of developing depression. Unsurprisingly, the standard American diet has been linked to higher incidence of depressive signs. The Mediterranean diet has also been studied in adolescents, and when adherence to the diet is high, they reported being happier, with higher self-confidence. Now that is living well!

THE GOLDEN RULES
OF MEDITERRANEAN LIVING

Whether you're on Spain's Costa del Sol or the Turkish Riviera, there's something about the confluence of sun, soil, and sea around the Mediterranean that sets the scene for great food, a slower pace, and healthy living. Before we dive into weight loss in chapter 2, it's worth keeping in mind the main tenets of Mediterranean living.

1. **Focus on fresh foods.** Fill your grocery basket with a colorful array of veggies, fruits, beans, nuts, seeds, and dairy, along with smaller servings of seafood, eggs, and poultry.

2. **Stay active.** Keeping active is so ingrained in Italian life that they have a name for the time-honored evening stroll: *la passeggiata*. Find ways to keep moving in your daily life: park the car a little farther, take the stairs instead of the elevator, or play with your kids at the park.

3. **Rest and relax.** Siesta time sees Spaniards share food with family and sometimes even take a short nap. Your days may not be quite so leisurely, but you should still find time to relax and reduce stress, be it picking up a good book, catching up with friends, or eating dinner with loved ones.

4. **Live to eat well.** Mediterranean eating does away with the idea of good food as a guilty pleasure. The "live to eat well" philosophy means putting mealtime at the heart of everyday life and savoring quality food.

5. **Eat to live long.** It's no coincidence that countries like Spain, Italy, and Israel have some of the longest life expectancies on Earth. By following an "eat to live long" approach, you, too, can manage your weight and improve your long-term health.

CHAPTER 2

Tackling Weight Loss

◇◇◇◇◇◇◇◇◇◇◇◇

Before we dive into this chapter, I want to congratulate you on deciding to choose sensible eating over fad dieting. As we've seen, good nutrition and positive lifestyle habits are better for you and give better results than yo-yo dieting. Weight loss starts in the kitchen, and you've heard it time and time again: You can't outrun a bad diet. That means that when nutrition comes first, you are well on your way to losing weight in a safe, healthy, and enjoyable manner.

Understanding Calories

We tend to think of "calorie" as a bad word, but it's not at all. A calorie is simply how we measure energy that's derived from food. Your body constantly requires calories to fuel your actions, whether you're walking, driving a car, or just breathing. Nutrients such as carbohydrates, fats, and proteins contain calories and are the body's main energy sources. The calories you eat are either converted to physical energy or stored within your body, sometimes as fat.

The basic tenet of weight loss is to burn more calories than you are taking in. As a general rule, you need to burn 3,500 calories more than you consume to shed one pound of fat—although many variables can affect this equation.

More often than not, weight gain is caused by eating more calories than you need, either in the absence of physical activity or with it. That does not mean that you need to massively restrict your calories, as in some crash diets. Decreasing your calories by a suitable number for your body size and sex, and then adding in physical activity, will help you achieve sustainable weight loss. The beauty of the Mediterranean diet is that by consuming healthy fats, lean proteins, and plant-based fiber, you are fueled by quality nutrients that leave you feeling satisfied long after you've eaten.

CALCULATE YOUR BMI

Body mass index, or BMI, is an indicator of body fat. This measure is meant to estimate whether you are underweight, at an appropriate weight, overweight, or obese. It's not a perfect measurement tool, but it is used to estimate your risk of disease, based on your height and weight.

To find your BMI, use this equation with weight in pounds and height in inches.

$$[\text{weight} \div (\text{height} \times \text{height})] \times 703$$

Let's see what this equation looks like in action. We'll take a hypothetical person who is five foot five (that's 65 inches) and weighs 160 pounds.

$$65 \times 65 = 4{,}225$$
$$160 \div 4{,}225 = 0.038 \times 703 = 26.6$$

This is how you interpret the number you get.

Underweight = less than 18.5
Normal weight = 18.5 to 24.9
Overweight = 25 to 29.9
Obesity = more than 30

Identify How Many Daily Calories You Need

To lose weight, it's important to be aware of how many calories you need to eat each day. Men and women have different calorie requirements, and body size will also affect your needs. The Dietary Guidelines for Americans (set by the U.S. Department of Health and Human Services) lists these general calorie requirements for men and women.

- Men (18 and over), moderately active: 2,400 to 2,800 calories
- Women (18 and over), moderately active: 1,800 to 2,200 calories

These calorie requirements are general recommendations for weight maintenance with moderate activity. The meal plan for this 21-day weight loss regimen is based on roughly 1,650 calories per day with exercise five days a week. With this meal plan and exercise schedule, you should expect to lose one pound a week. If you are not exercising, feel free to reduce your calorie intake to 1,500 calories to ensure you are able to get all the nutrients you need. This is the approach I have successfully used with my clients. Always remember, the weight did not come on quickly, so give yourself time to lose it.

Of course, you may need more or fewer calories based on your age, height, weight, and sex. For a more detailed estimate of your individual calorie needs, the National Institutes of Health Body Weight Planner is a great tool for estimating calories for weight loss (you can find it at NIDDK.NIH.gov/bwp).

This is not a starvation diet or an elimination diet. Drastically reducing calories is not a sustainable method for weight loss. If you're hungry, eat. Stick to a healthy snack option in chapter 6 (page 75) to satisfy your hunger. All of the recipes in this book have nutritional information, so if you need to add more calories, these recipes will show you a healthy way to do so.

It's worth noting that if you don't eat enough calories, you won't lose weight and you'll be miserable. Drastic calorie restriction may work for the short term, but most people find it unsustainable and the weight comes right back, according to 2018 research published in *Healthcare*.

When looking at calories and how they relate to weight loss, always reach for foods that are nutrient dense. This means the food offers more nutrients relative to the energy (calories) it provides. For example, 100 calories of nuts are more nutrient dense than 100 calories of gummy bears.

At the end of the day, what's important is that you follow a healthy eating pattern that feels comfortable for you. It is not in the Mediterranean lifestyle to count calories, but rather to pay attention to how your body feels. Eat when you're hungry, stop when you're comfortably full. Use calories as a guide to learn about the calorie content of foods, so you can make decisions about how to eat for a lifetime.

WHY FIBER IS YOUR FRIEND

The Mediterranean diet contains a colorful array of fiber-rich foods such as fruits, vegetables, beans, and nuts—which is good news for weight loss.

Fiber refers to carbohydrates that cannot be digested by the gut. There are two types: soluble, which attracts water and turns to a gel that slows down digestion; and insoluble, which adds bulk to your diet. Importantly, both types are low in calories and leave you feeling full longer. Fiber also feeds billions of good bacteria in your gut, which helps regulate weight through hormonal, neural, and metabolic processes in the body. All of these factors were borne out by a 2019 study published in the *Journal of Nutrition*, which found that fiber helps individuals lose weight independently of any other nutrient.

Women should aim for at least 25 grams of fiber per day, and men 38 grams per day. When following a plant-forward eating pattern like the Mediterranean diet, you should comfortably exceed these targets.

Portion Control

Eating at a restaurant in the Mediterranean is much different from dining out in the United States. The number one difference is portion size. The Mediterranean diet allows for all foods, if you want them. They are just not eaten in excess. This concept may be the most challenging part of following this diet pattern.

In some ways, it takes some habit-breaking and expectation management to understand proper portion sizes. Once you get it down, though, it will be the key to your weight loss. Check out the graphic on page 15 for serving sizes—no fancy measurement tools are required. There are no serving sizes for fresh fruits and veggies; that's because they will fill the majority of your diet.

While all the recipes in this book are portion-controlled, if you are creating your own meals, make sure half your plate is filled with vegetables, as it will greatly enhance your weight loss and your health. Then, stick to the serving sizes in the recipes of proteins, dairy, starches and starchy vegetables, such as potatoes and corn. As long as you are filling your plate with all of these foods, you will not feel deprived.

SERVING SIZES FOR COMMON FOODS

It can be helpful—and eye opening—to be aware of the portions you eat. Here are some serving size guidelines to follow:

FIST		¾ cup	Rice	150
			Pasta	150
			Potatoes	150
PALM		4 ounces	Lean meat	160
			Fish	160
			Poultry	160
HANDFUL		1 ounce	Nuts	170
			Raisins	85
THUMB		1 ounce	Peanut butter	170
			Hard cheese	100

THE BALANCED PLATE

Being on a Mediterranean diet doesn't have to mean a half-empty plate. Go ahead, fill it up! Before you start scooping, though, picture how you will fill your plate. A balanced plate is one that provides the right ratio of foods, and looks like the graphic below.

Good protein sources include fish, poultry, and lean meat that is grilled, baked, or broiled. Vegetables should fill half your plate, with fruit for dessert. Your starches on this diet include peas, beans, pasta, potatoes, sweet potatoes, butternut squash, and whole grains, such as whole-grain bread, quinoa, and farro. Stick to appropriate portion sizes of higher-calorie but healthy foods, such as nuts, avocados, and olive oil.

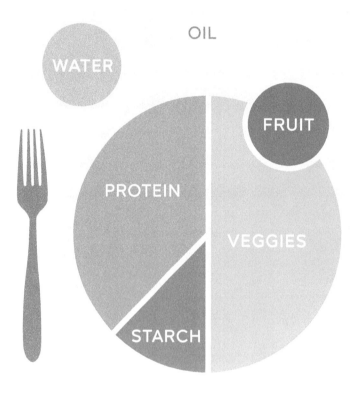

A Holistic Approach

The Mediterranean diet is truly a lifestyle choice. This doesn't mean you must eat only Mediterranean-style meals for the rest of your life. It simply means that the lifestyle principles that guide you on this 21-day plan are habits you adopt for a lifetime of healthy living. This plan will lead you step-by-step in how to seamlessly make little changes throughout your day. Eventually these little changes will help you achieve your bigger health goals. Recall the four pillars of the Mediterranean lifestyle that are all incorporated into this book. They are:

- Nutrition
- Exercise
- Relaxation
- Sleep

Nutrition

Reading this book shows your commitment to make nutrition a priority. Of all of the pillars, nutrition is the most important to master early. Research has shown that trying to change just the amount of carbohydrate or fat or protein in your diet does not lead to successful weight loss. Simply getting caught up in the importance of one macronutrient is not necessary—and not productive. Your focus should be on increasing the overall quality of your diet, reducing portion sizes, reducing the number of calories you eat, and increasing the amount of fiber you consume.

Exercise

While it is possible to lose weight by simply changing what you eat, if you exercise and build lean body mass (muscle), you will accelerate your weight loss and reap all of the associated health benefits. The American College of Sports Medicine recommends 150 to 250 minutes of exercise each week for modest weight loss (four to six pounds per month), but when exercise is consistently increased from the minimum amount to 225 minutes a week, weight loss accelerates.

The 21-day exercise program outlined in the next chapter takes a moderate approach of 180 minutes (three hours) of exercise per week. This allows you to start slightly above the minimum recommendation and gives you room for growth as you get stronger. This does not mean your exercise has to be hard—you just have to get your body moving. I will share with you a variety of cardio and strength exercises in chapter 3 so you can find the ones that best suit you.

Relaxation

It has been well established that chronic stress (the kind that sticks around) may have a significant impact on your weight. According to research published in 2018 in *Current Obesity Reports*, some people are more susceptible to the effects of stress, and for those individuals, stress makes them hungry and crave foods that are energy-dense—or to use a more familiar term, "comfort food." Stress can also impair your immune system, increase inflammation, and raise your blood pressure.

To decrease your stress, you need to identify what your stressors are in the first place. Only then can you take the steps to drive the stress out of your life—or at least reduce it. Here are some specific, practical, and achievable strategies for managing your stress.

EXERCISE. It's not just a cliché; exercise actually helps reduce your stress hormone, cortisol, and makes you feel energized and more positive when you are done. Some find it helpful to use a repetitive solo exercise that doesn't take a lot of thinking, to help clear the mind and zone out, and others find that exercising with friends is a joyful and fun experience.

MEDITATE. This can be as simple as closing your eyes and taking some deep breaths several times a day, finding free meditations on a video- or music-streaming service, or downloading a meditation app and dedicating more time to relaxation.

KEEP A GRATITUDE JOURNAL. In times of stress, it can be hard to see all of the good in your life. Write down what you are thankful for every day, and take the time to reflect on what you've written.

LAUGH. There is power in laughter. If you can't find someone to make you laugh, turn on a good comedy or get lost in a funny book. Either way, those giggles will help calm your stress.

Sleep

You should never underestimate the power of sleep. If you don't get enough, you wish you had more. You can think of sleep as the automatic update that happens to your body as you rest. It's when your body takes the time to heal. People who do not get enough sleep or have irregular sleep patterns have a higher risk for heart disease, type 2 diabetes, stroke, and high blood pressure.

Sleep can also affect your weight. Not getting enough sleep messes with your appetite hormones, meaning your hunger hormones go up. So that late-night snacking is not just boredom; your body is probably telling you to go to sleep.

How much sleep do you need? The National Institutes of Health recommend seven to eight hours every night for optimal health. If you have trouble getting enough, a few easy lifestyle changes can help.

- Get outside and/or exercise during the day. Both can help you sleep better at night.
- Find a way to de-stress before bedtime. Put the phone away, take a hot bath, read a book—whatever helps you unwind.
- Do not eat dinner within two hours of bedtime, which can cause indigestion or heartburn and lead to less restful sleep.

Identify Bad Habits

We all have bad habits. Bad lifestyle habits can keep you from hitting your weight loss goals. If you've tried to lose weight before, you can probably name one or two bad habits off the top of your head. Here are some of the bad habits I've seen most often with clients. They don't seem big, but when combined with others, they are goal killers.

SKIPPING MEALS: This is a mistake I see often with clients, and one that is not necessary for weight loss. You might hear that fasting or not eating breakfast is the way to lose weight because you naturally reduce your calories or it helps regulate your blood sugar. The truth is, your body likes food and your brain craves it. We've all been hangry before. Eating regular meals that are full of all three macronutrients (protein, carbohydrate, and fat) and fiber is the best way to regulate your eating. Skipping meals only leads to overcompensation at some point. You'll see research that supports one way or the other, but it ultimately comes down to making healthy choices at all meals.

NOT EATING ENOUGH. A client of mine once came to me because, even though she was eating a healthy diet, she still couldn't lose weight. Once we identified that she wasn't eating enough, she started to feel stronger, have more energy, and—you guessed it—lose weight. This may seem counterintuitive, given that so many weight-loss plans recommend very low-calorie meals. But these just leave you tired, hungry, and prone to overeating the next time you open the refrigerator. The goal is to change the quality of your diet, increase your fiber, add physical activity, and eat an appropriate number of calories for your body size.

EATING OUT TOO MUCH. Eating out at restaurants, take-out places, and fast-food chains isn't doing you any favors. You aren't able to control what's in your food, and that makes it tough to know how many calories you are eating. The portion sizes are much larger than what you need, as well, and we tend to clean our plate rather than take some home. Restaurant foods also tend to be energy-dense foods, not nutrient-dense foods. That means you are getting more calories relative to the density of the nutrients. That said, it doesn't have to be all or nothing: Balance your home-cooked meals with a meal out once every two weeks to give yourself a break from cooking.

NOT EXERCISING. It is possible to lose weight without exercise, but if you really want to see results, it's time to get moving. There's no rule that says you have to go out and run a 5K to lose weight; all forms of physical activity work for weight loss. Exercise, depending on the intensity, has the potential to burn calories for several hours after you do it, because your metabolism is still revved up. Use that to your advantage for weight loss.

Use the 21-day plan weekly habit tracker to break bad habits and cultivate good ones.

Set SMART Goals

If you have tried to lose weight before, it's possible you had a goal weight in mind at the beginning of your diet. This is typically the most useful way to track your progress. But you are free to have other goals as well, such as having more energy, lowering your blood pressure, and improving your blood sugar levels.

A SMART goals checklist will help you clarify your ideas, focus your efforts, and increase your chances of success. Consider whether your goals fit the following SMART criteria.

SPECIFIC. A good goal includes specific details. For example, a goal to simply exercise more is not specific, but a goal to exercise for 30 minutes before leaving for work is specific. You are saying what you will do, how long you will do it, and when you will do it. Getting specific about how you want to improve your lifestyle is vital to keeping you on track.

MEASURABLE. To track your progress, a goal must be measurable. If you plan on exercising five days a week and you do it, then you reached your goal. If you plan on getting 25 grams of fiber per day and you eat 28 grams of fiber, you reached and exceeded your goal. Keeping a journal or tracking your goals in an app is a great way to see if you are reaching them daily.

ATTAINABLE. Are your goals realistic? You want to set challenging goals for yourself, but not so challenging that they are impossible to meet. Be honest with yourself when setting your goals and make sure they are achievable. For example, when you decide on the calorie count that is appropriate for you, is it attainable?

RELEVANT. A relevant goal is one that is set with your desired results in mind. For example, for your overarching goal of weight loss, it would not be relevant to set a goal about improving your cooking skills. While that may be an outcome of adopting a Mediterranean lifestyle, you don't have to be a good cook to lose weight. A more relevant goal would be to try four or five new healthy recipes each week.

TIME-BASED. How much time are you willing to give yourself to get this done? For example, your time-based goal could be: "By the end of the 21-day program, I will be in the habit of exercising at least five days a week and getting 25 grams of fiber in my diet every day."

When setting goals for weight loss, it is really tempting to go for slimming down fast. It can feel so rewarding. But often that weight doesn't stay off. Gradually adding better daily habits will keep you on track for sustainable weight loss. Losing one to two pounds a week is my gold standard for long-term weight loss, but be mindful that weight loss will happen at different rates for every person.

Good work should not come without reward. When you hit short-term goals, no matter how small, find ways to reward yourself that do not involve treats or "cheat days." Here are some ideas for rewarding yourself that work well in your new lifestyle.

- Buy new workout shoes/workout clothes/workout equipment.
- Take a trip to a new farmers' market.
- Give yourself time to read a book in a quiet spot.
- Get a massage/manicure/pedicure.
- Buy yourself flowers.

CHAPTER 3

Your Exercise Routine

◇◇◇◇◇◇◇◇◇◇◇◇◇◇◇◇◇◇◇◇◇

Now it's time to take a closer look at the role exercise will play in your Mediterranean lifestyle and for weight loss. Don't worry, the 21-day plan doesn't call for extreme workouts, just purposeful and enjoyable activity. In this chapter, there are examples of exercises that will work your entire body, build lean muscle, and help rev up your metabolism. You will set your routine and learn the importance of hydration and how it will enhance your workouts and weight loss.

Resetting Your Mindset

Exercise is often one of the commitments that seems the hardest, but changing your mindset about it can help sustain you through this 21-day plan and for the rest of your life. I always say that we make the time for things that are important, and making the time for exercise is challenging but never impossible.

Research shows that regularly working out is one of the most important things you can do for your health. In fact, many medical providers now prescribe exercise as a treatment alongside good nutrition and medication; sometimes even as an alternative to medication. Being physically fit helps improve blood sugar control, lower blood pressure, and improve bone and muscle strength, among many other benefits.

Regular exercise is also one of the best things you can do to take care of your mental well-being. It has been shown to reduce anxiety, help you sleep better, reduce feelings of sadness and depression, and give you a more positive outlook overall.

The 21-Day Workout Plan

Your workout plan includes a mix of the two types of exercise recommended for weight loss: cardiovascular (cardio) and strength training. Let's take a closer look.

CARDIO. Also known as aerobic exercise, cardio refers to activities like walking, running, and biking that get you moving over a sustained period of time and raise your heart rate. This puts you into the target zone where you burn calories and fat.

STRENGTH TRAINING. This refers to exercises that make your muscles work harder than usual. It may include using weights for exercises like lunges and shoulder presses, but also includes exercises that require nothing but the weight of your body, such as push-ups. This is also essential on the plan because these kinds of exercises will help increase how many calories you burn every day. Lean muscle, as opposed to fat, has a higher metabolic rate, so the more muscle you have, the more calories you burn at rest.

For the 21-day plan, you will work out five days each week. You will do four 30-minute cardio sessions and two 30-minute strength training workouts, with two days of rest. Here is what a week's worth of exercise might look like.

MON	TUE	WED	THU	FRI	SAT	SUN
Strength training	Cardio	Rest	Cardio	Rest	Cardio and strength training	Cardio

If you aren't doing any exercise right now, don't worry; this routine is more than doable. As you get stronger and increase your stamina, you may even find you want to increase the time you spend exercising throughout the week. For example, you can take your cardio to five days a week or add in light physical activity (taking a walk, playing outside with kids, gardening) on your rest days. Go for it, but don't feel that you have to blast out of the gates with exercise just yet.

Before you start the program, be sure to have a conversation with your doctor to ensure that any preexisting conditions do not hinder your ability to exercise. If you are already exercising, feel free to bump up the time and intensity of your workouts.

GETTING THE MOST OUT OF WORKOUTS

Making exercise a regular part of your schedule may seem difficult at first, but there are many things you can do to make it as enjoyable and effective as possible.

Choose the time of day that works for you. Maybe you're a morning person, or maybe you're a night owl. Choose the time of day that you are most likely to stick with.

Alternate and vary your workouts. If you are adding strength training to your routine, give your muscles 24 to 48 hours of rest before another strength training session. Add some variation to your cardio, too. Try a workout video at home or take a brisk walk to change things up.

Don't work out on a full stomach. Exercising on a full stomach can cause you a lot of discomfort, from feeling sluggish to having cramps. Hold off on your workout for at least two hours after a meal.

Put on the tunes. Music can help amplify your mood and may help you get more out of your workout by increasing the time you spend exercising.

Find an accountability buddy. Having someone to work out and talk about your meals with is a huge motivator to stay on track—and will push you to reach your goals together. Whether it's a friend, spouse, or loved one, having a person with whom you articulate your goals will help you reach them faster.

Cardio Exercises

In this section, I discuss several different types of exercise so that you can choose the ones that suit you best. These will make up the five days of workouts each week, as shown on the table on page 26.

Cardio can take many different forms, and contrary to what many people might believe, this type of exercise does not have to be high impact. If you have issues with impact activity, choose walking, cycling, or swimming, or use low-impact equipment, such as an elliptical machine or an exercise bike.

WALKING. You can walk briskly outdoors or on a treadmill. It is an excellent way to get your heart rate up without putting a lot of stress on your joints.

JOGGING AND RUNNING. If you want to take your walks to the next level, start with a slow jog and work up to a faster pace. Jogging and running are excellent cardiovascular workouts, when you're ready for the challenge.

SWIMMING. Swimming is an ideal low-impact, total body exercise. Swim laps and slowly progress to a faster pace and longer time in the water.

BIKING. Going for a bike ride isn't just for kids. Grab that helmet and get on the road for some good cardio training that isn't hard on your joints.

JUMPING JACKS, HIGH KNEES, AND JUMP ROPE. These old-school exercises can really get your heart pumping, especially when combined with other cardio activities.

Aim for 30 minutes of cardio in each session—but it doesn't all have to be the same thing. For example, you could walk and also do jumping jacks.

Strength Training Exercises

There are numerous strength training options, which I have divided into four categories: full body, upper body, lower body, and core.

For each of your strength training workouts, start by doing as much as you can and work up to a set of 10 repetitions of each exercise. Rest for 30 to 60 seconds between each set, and do a total of three sets. (So that's 30 reps total, with a brief rest after each 10.)

Full Body

BURPEE

Start by standing with your feet hip-width apart. Lower yourself into a squat. Place your hands on the floor in front of you and shift your weight forward. Jump or walk your feet back into the top of a push-up, keeping your abdominal muscles (abs) engaged and making sure your body creates a straight line. Jump or walk your feet back toward your hands and return to the bottom of the squat. Jump or stand up, reaching your arms straight overhead. This is one repetition.

MOUNTAIN CLIMBER

Start on the floor in a push-up position. Maintain a slight arch in your back and raise one knee toward your chest. Pause, return to the starting position, and repeat with your other leg. This is one repetition. Alternate legs until you have completed all your reps.

Upper Body

PUSH-UP

Start by kneeling on the floor with your hands directly under your shoulders. Lift your body into a plank position with your weight evenly distributed on your hands and feet. Draw your shoulder blades in, while keeping your elbows close to your body. Lower your body until your chest touches the floor. Make sure your abs and glutes (your backside) are still engaged, and exhale as you push yourself up, in one straight line, to the starting position. This is one repetition. If this is too challenging, keep your knees on the floor while performing the push-up.

TRICEPS DIP

Start by sitting on the floor with a step, bench, or sturdy chair directly behind you. With your knees slightly bent and your feet planted firmly on the floor, grab the edge of the elevated surface behind you, and place your hands on it slightly wider than shoulder-width apart. Bend your arms to a 90-degree angle, keeping your elbows close to your body. Brace your abs and straighten your arms, pushing through your heels. Lower yourself back down to a seated position. This is one repetition.

SHOULDER PRESS

Start by standing with your feet hip-width apart and a dumbbell (or resistance band anchored by your feet) in each hand. Raise the weights to shoulder height and bring your elbows to a 90-degree angle. Brace your abs and extend through your elbows to raise the weights together directly above your head. Pause at the top and then slowly return to the starting position. This is one repetition.

Lower Body

SQUAT

Start by standing with your feet hip-width apart or slightly wider. Extend your hands straight out in front of you for balance. Brace your abs and sit back and down as if you're sitting on an imaginary chair. Keep your chest up and look straight ahead. Go as far down as you can without dropping your chest. Once you reach your depth, press through your heels and spring back into the standing position, squeezing your glutes at the top. This counts as one repetition.

LUNGE

Start by standing with your feet a bit wider than hip-width apart. Brace your abs and take a big step forward with your left foot. Make sure your knees, hips, and shoulders all face forward. Keep your chest up and your abs engaged, and sink straight down until your left knee makes a 90-degree angle and your right knee is pointing straight down toward the floor. Make sure your left knee does not go past your toes. Shift your weight onto the ball of your right foot as you push back up, and step back into the starting position. This counts as one repetition.

GLUTE BRIDGE

Start by lying on your back on the floor with your hands by your sides and your knees bent. Your feet should be hip-width apart. With your weight in your heels, breathe out as you lift your hips off the floor while keeping your back straight. Hold at the top for a few seconds and then slowly lower back to the floor as you breathe in. This counts as one repetition.

Variation: Perform the exercise on one leg at a time with the other leg straight up in the air.

Core

PLANK

Start by lying on your stomach on the floor. Place your forearms on the floor with your elbows aligned directly under your shoulders, forming a 90-degree angle. Raise your knees off the floor, supporting your weight on your toes and forearms. Your body should form a straight line from your head to your feet. Set your gaze at a point on the floor about a foot in front of you, and make sure your neck is in-line with the rest of your body. Breathe as you hold this position for as long as you can, squeezing your core and glutes, then return to the starting position. This counts as one set. Work up to a 30-second hold before resting. Repeat two more times.

BICYCLE CRUNCH

Start by lying on your back on the floor. Bring your knees to your chest (your feet will be off the floor) and place your hands behind your head, interlocking your fingers. Lift your shoulders off the floor, tighten your abs, and tuck your chin into your chest. Touch the inside of your right arm to the inside of your left thigh while straightening your right leg. Alternate and touch the inside of your left arm to the inside of your right thigh while straightening your left leg. This counts as one repetition.

HOLLOW ROCK

Start by lying on your back on the floor. Contract your abs while pressing your lower back into the floor. With your legs straight and toes pointed, raise your legs off the floor a couple of inches. Straighten your arms above your head and raise them off the floor so they are aligned with your ears. Keeping your lower back on the floor and abs engaged, rock back and forth for 10 seconds without allowing the shape to break, then lower your arms and legs to the floor. This counts as one repetition.

COMMON EXERCISE MYTHS

Many people think they have to lift heavy weights or run miles to lose weight. There are lots of myths out there, so let's dispel a few to assist you in your wellness journey.

Myth 1: More time doing cardio means more weight loss.

Doing plenty of cardio will for sure help you lose weight, but it's not all about cardio. To keep that calorie burn going and keep your metabolism high, you need to build muscle as well. So, a healthy mix of cardio and strength training will help you lose weight and keep it off.

Myth 2: Doing core work will get rid of my muffin top.

Unfortunately, you can't spot-reduce. More core work will strengthen your core, but it won't get rid of any fat around the midsection on its own. That will take both cardio and overall strength training.

Especially when you first start exercising, taking rest days is essential. Two days of rest during the week should work just fine. It is extremely important you give your body some time off and get enough sleep to repair and rejuvenate for the next day.

Myth 4: Exercise was never meant to be enjoyable.
Exercise should make you feel good and definitely should not make you feel any pain. It can be difficult when your heart starts pumping and you get tired, but controlling your breathing and having faith in your body can go a long way to helping you finish a workout.

Stay Hydrated

Good hydration is one of the keys to your success in losing weight and having the energy to exercise. Did you know that losing only 1 to 2 percent of your body's water weight can cause a detectable decrease in performance when you exercise?

Staying hydrated is also critical for your eating plan. When you are dehydrated, it's easy to confuse feelings of thirst for hunger. So even though you think you have a craving for a snack, you may actually need something to drink.

It is recommended that women drink about 11 (8-ounce) cups of water a day and that men drink about 15 cups a day. You will need even more water on the days you exercise, especially if you sweat a lot.

Water should always be your first choice for fluid, but eating foods high in water also counts toward your daily amount of water. Broth-based soups and fruits and vegetables high in water, such as watermelon, berries, cucumbers, and lettuce, are all good options. Carry a water bottle with you throughout the day as a reminder to drink water.

PIZZA WITH PESTO, MUSHROOMS, AND SPINACH; PAGE 113

CHAPTER 4

The 21-Day Plan

You are now ready to begin your 21-day Mediterranean diet weight loss plan! In this chapter, you'll find simple menus for each week using nutritious and delicious recipes from the book. You will also find healthy snack ideas, shopping lists, exercise charts for each week, and a healthy habit tracker. You have what it takes to begin this journey of healthy eating and exercise, so let's get started!

About the 21-Day Plan

This 21-day plan has not been designed as a restrictive diet for weight loss. It combines the "live to eat" philosophy of Mediterranean eating, in which food is a pleasurable and important part of daily life, with the "eat to live" mindset of filling your plate with all the right nutrients to enjoy lifelong good health.

The eating plan is designed for two people. The majority of the recipes make four servings, which allows for preportioned leftovers the next day. If you are cooking for a family, either adjust the recipe to fit your family or do not plan on having leftovers and try a different recipe for lunch. If you are eating solo, you can halve the quantities in the recipes.

On this plan you will be eating about 1,650 calories a day. With exercise added in for additional calorie burn, this should result in about one pound of weight loss per week. This calorie range is a general recommendation. Smaller women may need fewer calories and men and taller women may need slightly more, as I explained in chapter 2.

If you find that you are hungry between meals, don't worry. As your body uses more energy, it will naturally want to take in more calories. Your body likes to stay in equilibrium, which is why losing weight can feel hard. Healthy snacks are factored into the plan. Aiming for about 300 calories total each day from snacks will help keep hunger in check. Note that snacks are not included on the shopping lists, so be sure to add them each week.

Week One

This is it! You are ready to start. Everything comes together better with a plan, so take a few minutes to get yourself organized. This week, you should inventory your pantry to see what you already have and then go shopping for what you don't. Stick to your grocery list. Make sure you plan out what snacks you might want during the week and add those to your list. Fill out the Your Personal Trainer exercise table (page 43) and Habit Tracker (page 44) to keep yourself accountable, and stick to them.

Prep Ahead

Starting any new eating plan can be daunting and intimidating, but the more you plan ahead, the less you have to think about putting food on the table. If you want to do some prep before you start, you can make Monday's lunch on Sunday and cook extra farro for Tuesday's dinner. You can also prepare the snacks you want.

If you're packing lunches, pack the veggies separate from any dressings or vinaigrettes and dress your meal right before you eat it (unless otherwise specified). This will keep your vegetables crisp.

About the Shopping

Week 1's shopping list is going to look like a lot of ingredients, but remember this is every meal for an entire week for two people. Many of the ingredients you buy this first week will be used again in week 2 and week 3, so your shopping list will get shorter. Always check your refrigerator and pantry before you shop, so you don't double up on items.

Week One Shopping List

Beef, extra-lean (97%) ground
    (1½ pounds)
Chicken breasts, boneless, skinless
    (1 pound)
Chicken, ground (1 pound)
Cod fillet, fresh or frozen (8 ounces)
Salmon fillet, skin-on (1 pound)
Tuna, packed in olive oil,
    1 (5-ounce) can

Cheese, feta, 1 (4-ounce) block
Cheese, feta, crumbled (13 ounces)
Cheese, Parmesan, 1 (6-ounce) block
Cheese, part-skim ricotta (1⅓ cups)
Cheese, whole-milk mozzarella
    (4 ounces)
Eggs, large (5)
Milk, 2% (4 cups)
Yogurt, plain full-fat Greek (40 ounces)

Arugula, 1 (5-ounce) package
Avocado (1)
Baby spinach, 2 (10-ounce) bags
Bananas, small (2)
Bell pepper, green (1)
Berries, of choice (5 cups)
Blueberries (2 cups)
Carrots, large (5)
Cherries (2 cups)
Cucumber, English (1)
Cucumber, Persian (1)
Cucumber, small (3)
Dill (1 bunch)
Eggplant (1)
Field greens, 1 (10-ounce) bag
Fruit, of choice (8 pieces or 8 cups)
Garlic bulb (1)
Lemons (4)
Lettuce, iceberg or Bibb (1 head)
Mixed greens, 1 (10-ounce) bag

Onion, yellow or white, small (1)
Onions, red (5)
Parsley (1 bunch)
Tomatoes, large (6)
Tomatoes, vine-ripened (4)
Zucchini (1)
Zucchini, large (1)

Blueberries (2 cups)

Almonds, unsalted
Basil pesto
Dijon mustard
Olives, green
Olives, Kalamata
Pine nuts
Pistachios, unsalted
Pitas, whole-wheat
Walnuts

Black pepper
Breadcrumbs, seasoned
Cannellini beans, canned
Chickpeas, canned
Cinnamon, ground
Farro
Honey
Italian seasoning
Marinara sauce, jarred
Nonstick cooking spray
Oil, extra-virgin olive
Oregano, dried
Paprika, smoked
Salt, kosher
Sugar
Vinegar, balsamic
Vinegar, white wine

Week One Meal Plan

	BREAKFAST	LUNCH	DINNER
MON	Grab-and-Go Breakfast Pack (page 64)	Farro with Cucumbers, White Beans, and Lemon (page 109) + 1 medium piece or 1 cup fresh fruit per person	Weeknight Garlic and Lemon Baked Cod (page 129) + Weeknight Garden Salad with Vinaigrette (page 90) + 1 cup berries per person
TUE	Grab-and-Go Breakfast Pack (page 64)	Leftovers from Monday	Roasted Vegetable and Chickpea Bowl with Farro (page 110)
WED	Fruit and Honey Yogurt Parfait (page 61)	Leftovers from Tuesday	Pesto Salmon with Pine Nuts and Lemon (page 137) + Classic Greek Salad (page 91)
THU	Make-Ahead Muesli (page 65) + ½ cup 2% milk per person	Leftovers from Wednesday + 1 medium piece or 1 cup fresh fruit per person	Chicken Burger Lettuce Wraps (page 147) + Parmesan Zucchini Fries (page 164)
FRI	Fruit and Honey Yogurt Parfait (page 61)	Leftovers from Thursday + 1 medium piece or 1 cup fresh fruit per person	Spanish-Style Meatballs in Tomato Sauce (page 153) + Honey-Roasted Carrots (page 167) + Whipped Ricotta with Cherries, Honey, and Pistachios (page 179)
SAT	Banana, Blueberry, Almond Smoothie (page 60)	Leftovers from Friday	Chicken Gyro Bowl (page 150) + 1 cup fresh fruit per person
SUN	Leftover Make-Ahead Muesli + ½ cup 2% milk per person	Tuna, Avocado, and Cucumber Stuffed Pita (page 127)	Greek-Style Stuffed Tomatoes (page 155)

SNACKS TO ENJOY
THROUGHOUT THE 21 DAYS

To make your weight-loss journey easier, this meal plan allows for 300 calories of snacks per day so you don't go hungry between meals. I left the snacks off the meal plans so you could choose your own.

You're working out more, so that means your metabolism is revved up and that will naturally make you hungry. Don't derail your success by reaching for a candy bar or a bag of chips. Make nutrient-dense choices, like the snacks suggested here, and add them to the weekly shopping list.

Chapter 6 has recipes for 12 snacks. If you prefer, each of the following choices is about 150 calories.

- 20 almonds
- 14 walnut halves
- 50 pistachios
- 1 large banana
- 4 cups air-popped popcorn
- ½ cup Greek yogurt with ¼ cup raspberries
- 1 cup baby carrots with 2 tablespoons hummus
- 1 cup edamame
- 1 sliced plum with ¼ cup ricotta cheese
- 1 cup raspberries and 1 mozzarella cheese stick
- 1 medium apple and 10 small olives, green or black
- 2 cups celery sticks with 2 tablespoons chive cream cheese

Remember that fruits and vegetables high in water content are low in calories. These should be your first choice for snacking. Bananas, oranges, apples, carrots, and snack peppers all travel well, so they are perfect for snacking on the go.

Your Personal Trainer

Below is a proposed exercise plan for week 1. Fill in the table with the cardio and strength training exercises from chapter 3 that you plan to do this week. Of course, you are free to draw up your own table if you wish to work out on different days. What's important is that you exercise on five days, doing four 30-minute cardio sessions and two 30-minute strength training workouts (with two days of rest).

M	T	TH	SAT	S
Full Body:	Cardio:	Cardio:	Cardio:	Cardio:
Upper Body:			Full Body:	
Lower Body:			Upper Body:	
Core:			Lower Body:	
			Core:	

Habit Tracker

It's important to make healthy lifestyle choices in addition to dietary changes. Make a list of healthy habits you want to maintain over the next three weeks—such as drinking a glass of water every hour, or getting seven to eight hours of sleep each night—and mark the days where you succeeded.

HABIT	M	T	W	TH	F	SAT	S
Drink 11 glasses of water	X		X	X		X	X

Week Two

Great work making it through week 1! Heading into week 2, remember to stay on track with your exercise and eating plan. Make sure you are planning out snacks and keeping them with you if hunger strikes. Drink water. Keep a water bottle with you and refill it throughout the day to stay hydrated to keep you powered up through your workouts.

Check the box on page 42 for snack inspiration, or head to chapter 6 for more ideas, keeping in mind that the meal plan allows for 300 calories per day for snacks.

Always keep in mind the four pillars of the 21-day plan: good nutrition, physical activity, relaxation, and sleep. Go back to pages 17-19 in chapter 2 to refresh your mind on these pillars if you need to.

Week Two Shopping List

Chicken breasts, boneless, skinless
(1 pound)
Chicken, rotisserie (1 pound)
Sausage, spicy Italian turkey (8 ounces)
Shrimp, fresh or frozen (12 ounces)
Tilapia fillets (1 pound)

Cheese, crumbled feta (4 ounces)
Cheese, Parmesan, 1 (6-ounce) block
Cheese, sliced mozzarella (4 ounces)
Eggs, large (4)
Milk, 2% (½ gallon)
Heavy cream (½ pint)
Yogurt, plain full-fat Greek (40 ounces)

Arugula (8 cups)
Avocados (2)
Baby spinach, 1 (10-ounce) bag
Bananas, small (4)
Basil (1 bunch)
Berries, of choice (7 cups)
Carrot, large (1)
Cucumber (1)
Cucumber, small (3)
Dill (1 bunch)
Eggplant (1)
Fruit, of choice (2 cups)
Fruit, of choice (4 pieces or 4 cups)
Garlic bulb (1)
Lemons (2)

Lime (1)
Mixed greens, 3 (10-ounce) bags
Onion, red, large (1)
Onions, red, small (4)
Onions, yellow or white (2)
Parsley (1 bunch)
Pears (4)
Potatoes, Yukon Gold or red (1 pound)
Radishes (1 bunch)
Scallions (2)
Snack peppers (4)
Tomatoes, cherry (2 pints)
Tomatoes, large (8)
Zucchini (1)
Zucchini, small (1)

Blueberries, frozen (4 cups)

Almonds, unsalted
Basil pesto
Dijon mustard
English muffins, whole-wheat
Olives, Kalamata
Tomatoes, sun-dried in olive oil, jarred
Walnuts

Black beans, canned
Black pepper
Chickpeas, canned
Cinnamon, ground

Cumin, ground

Honey

Italian seasoning

Oats, gluten-free old-fashioned rolled

Oil, canola

Oil, extra-virgin olive

Paprika

Paprika, smoked

Pasta, small shape of choice

Pasta, spaghetti

Red pepper flakes

Rice, short-grain, such as bomba
   or arborio

Salt, kosher

Sugar

Sugar, brown

Tomatoes, fire-roasted, canned

Turmeric, ground

Vanilla extract

Vinegar, white wine

Week Two Meal Plan

	BREAKFAST	LUNCH	DINNER
MON	Banana, Blueberry, Almond Smoothie (page 60)	Leftovers from week 1 Sunday + 1 cup berries per person	Turkey Sausage and Pasta Soup (page 100) + Weeknight Garden Salad with Vinaigrette (page 90)
TUE	Caprese Breakfast Sandwich (page 68)	Leftovers from Monday + 1 medium piece or 1 cup fresh fruit per person	Creamy Sun-Dried Tomato Chicken (page 151) + Weeknight Garden Salad with Vinaigrette (page 90)
WED	Banana, Blueberry, Almond Smoothie (page 60)	Leftovers from Tuesday	Roasted Chickpea and Feta Salad (page 104) + 1 cup berries per person
THU	Caprese Breakfast Sandwich (page 68)	Leftovers from Wednesday	Creamy Pesto Chicken and Arugula (page 146) + Patatas Bravas with Paprika Yogurt (page 172)
FRI	Fruit and Honey Yogurt Parfait (page 61)	Leftovers from Thursday	Tomato Basil Tilapia in Olive Oil (page 134) + Weeknight Garden Salad with Vinaigrette (page 90)
SAT	Fruit and Honey Yogurt Parfait (page 61)	Leftovers from Friday + 1 medium piece or 1 cup fresh fruit per person	Smoky Rice and Beans with Avocado and Lime (page 108) + Roasted Eggplant, Zucchini, and Red Onion (page 170) + Vanilla Baked Pears (page 180)
SUN	Spanish-Style Scrambled Eggs (page 71)	Leftovers from Saturday	Spaghetti Aglio e Olio with Shrimp (page 139) + 1 cup fresh fruit per person + Leftover Vanilla Baked Pears

Your Personal Trainer

M	T	W	TH	F	SAT	S
Full Body:	Cardio:	R E S T	Cardio:	R E S T	Cardio:	Cardio:
Upper Body:					Full Body:	
Lower Body:					Upper Body:	
Core:					Lower Body:	
					Core:	

Habit Tracker

HABIT	M	T	W	TH	F	SA	S
Drink 11 glasses of water	X		X	X		X	X

Week Three

Bravo for making it to week 3! This is your last week of the 21-day plan, so make it a good one. Your meal plan uses a few new spices to give you some variety in your meals. Travel around the Mediterranean in your kitchen. Your meal plan ensures you have a quick but healthy breakfast to keep you powered up as your day begins, and continue to use leftovers as you wish. Keep making smart choices for snacks, and by the end of the week your clothes may be feeling a little looser.

Week Three Shopping List

Beef, extra-lean (97%) ground
    (1 pound)
Chicken breasts, boneless, skinless
    (1 pound)
Salmon fillet (1 pound)
Sausage links, Italian chicken (4)
Tilapia fillets (1 pound)

Butter, unsalted (1 stick)
Cheese, crumbled feta (8 ounces)
Cheese, mozzarella (4 ounces)
Cheese, Parmesan, 1 (8-ounce) block
Cheese, ricotta (4 ounces)
Cream cheese, chive,
    1 (4-ounce) package
Eggs, large (14)
Milk, 2% (½ gallon)

Baby spinach, 3 (15-ounce) bags
Bananas, small (2)
Bell pepper, green, large (1)
Bell pepper, red, large (1)
Berries, of choice (2 cups)
Blueberries (1 cup)
Broccoli (2 large heads)
Carrots (1 pound)
Celery (1 bunch)
Cilantro (1 bunch)

Cucumber, Persian or English (1)
Dill (1 bunch)
Fruit (s), of choice (6 cups)
Garlic bulb (1)
Grapes (1 cup)
Lemons (5)
Lettuce, iceberg (1 head)
Mint (1 bunch)
Mushrooms, white button (8 ounces)
Onion, red (1)
Onions, yellow or white (3)
Onions, yellow or white, small (2)
Oranges (4)
Raspberries (1 cup)
Scallion (1)
Snack peppers (4)
Tomato, large (1)
Tomatoes, cherry (2 pounds)

Blueberries, frozen (2 cups)
Spinach, frozen, 2 (10-ounce) packages

Almonds, unsalted, sliced
Almonds, unsalted, whole
Basil pesto
Bread slices, hearty whole-wheat
English muffins, whole-wheat
Pitas, whole-wheat
Walnuts

Black pepper
Broth, low-sodium vegetable
Cannellini beans, canned
Chickpeas, canned
Cinnamon, ground
Coriander, ground
Couscous
Cumin, ground
Flour, all-purpose
Flour, whole-wheat
Garlic powder
Honey

Italian seasoning
Nonstick cooking spray
Oil, extra-virgin olive
Oregano, dried
Paprika, smoked
Red pepper flakes
Salt, kosher
Sugar
Tomato paste, canned
Tomatoes, diced, canned
Tomatoes, fire-roasted, canned
Turmeric, ground

Week Three Meal Plan

	BREAKFAST	LUNCH	DINNER
MON	Mediterranean Eggs Breakfast Sandwich (page 70) + 1 orange per person	Leftovers from week 2 Sunday	Moroccan-Inspired Beef with Couscous (page 156) + Creamed Spinach with Parmesan (page 165)
TUE	Mediterranean Eggs Breakfast Sandwich (page 70) + 1 orange per person	Leftovers from Monday	Fast Minestrone (page 98) + Fattoush (page 94) + Lemon Granita (page 177)
WED	Leftover Make-Ahead Muesli (from week 1) + ½ cup 2% milk per person	Leftovers from Tuesday	Salmon and Broccoli with Lemon Dill Sauce (page 138) + 1 cup berries per person
THU	Crostini and Berry Plate with Feta-Ricotta Spread (page 63)	Leftovers from Wednesday + 1 medium piece or 1 cup fresh fruit per person	Italian Chicken Sausage and Peppers Skillet (page 148) + Cherry Tomatoes with Mozzarella and Basil Pesto (page 162) + Leftover Lemon Granita
FRI	Banana, Blueberry, Almond Smoothie (page 60)	Leftovers from Thursday	Pan-Seared Tilapia with Cilantro Gremolata (page 132) + Spicy Roasted Broccoli with Almonds (page 169)
SAT	Spanish-Style Scrambled Eggs (page 71) + 1 cup fresh fruit per person	Leftovers from Friday	Slow-Roasted Chicken and Chickpea Stew (page 149)
SUN	Mediterranean Eggs Breakfast Sandwich (page 70)	Leftovers from Saturday	Healthy Tuscan Quiche (page 120) + 1 medium piece or 1 cup fresh fruit per person

Your Personal Trainer

M	T	W	TH	F	SAT	S
Full Body:	Cardio:		Cardio:		Cardio:	Cardio:
Upper Body:					Full Body:	
Lower Body:					Upper Body:	
Core:					Lower Body:	
					Core:	

Habit Tracker

HABIT	M	T	W	TH	F	SAT	S
Drink 11 glasses of water	X		X	X		X	X

Beyond the First 21 Days

Sticking with any program is hard, and if you've made it through your 21-day plan, you deserve a huge round of applause. As you continue with your Mediterranean way of eating, you can create your own weekly menus with the recipes from this book. Keep exercising, but pay attention to your body. Rest when you need to and get active when you can. You might find that exercise is getting easier. If that's the case, increase your time enjoying physical activity or bump up the intensity. The Mediterranean lifestyle is all about living your best life.

Tackling Slow Progress

If you're not seeing the results you want, don't throw in the towel. Consistency is key, and with fluctuations in water weight throughout the month, you may not see that scale moving the way you'd like it to. One thing's for sure, though: You're getting healthier. Pay attention to how your mood has improved and whether you feel stronger. Here are some tips for tackling slow progress.

CHECK YOUR CALORIE NEEDS. If you aren't seeing any weight loss, go back and check to see how many calories you should be eating. The 21-day meal plan is set for around 1,650 calories each day. You may need slightly more than that. Do a double-check of your needs (see page 38 in chapter 3) and adjust accordingly.

PRACTICE GOOD SELF-CARE. Think back to the four pillars of the 21-day plan: nutrition, exercise, relaxation, and sleep. Remember to take some downtime for yourself to recharge. This means getting enough sleep, drinking enough water, and finding healthy ways to relieve stress. When the body is stressed, it likes to hold on to weight, not let it go.

GET CREATIVE WITH EXERCISE. If you're finding that you don't have enough time for exercise, break it up into smaller sessions. Three 10-minute sessions of an exercise day may be better for you. You can squeeze in cardio throughout the day and find creative ways to fit in short bursts of strength activity, such as:

· Do two minutes of squats while brushing your teeth.
· Perform calf raises while talking on the phone.
· Walk or ride a bike instead of taking the car for errands that are nearby.
· Do push-ups during TV commercial breaks.

Setting a Course for Lifelong Health

This plan is meant to get you started on a path for healthier living over a lifetime. After you reach your goal weight, you should continue to maintain the quality of your diet. If you want to continue to track your calories, go for it, but it's not necessary if the majority of your meals are filled with plant-based, unprocessed foods. Listen to your body's hunger cues and eat when you're hungry and stop when you're full. Eat slowly, drink water, and continue to exercise for your good health.

The Recipes

Breakfasts

Banana, Blueberry, Almond Smoothie

Serves 2 ◆ Prep time: 5 minutes

FEW INGREDIENTS ◆ GLUTEN-FREE ◆ UNDER 30 MINUTES ◆ VEGETARIAN

Getting enough protein at breakfast can be a real challenge. On busy mornings, I like to make a smoothie super quick and get going. Nuts, fruit, and dairy are all staples in the Mediterranean diet, and blending them all together unifies their health benefits. Almonds blend up surprisingly well in a blender. Add them first, so they get the first touch of the blender blades for a creamy smoothie.

30 unsalted almonds

2 small bananas

2 cups frozen blueberries

2 cups 2% milk

1. In a blender, place the almonds, bananas, blueberries, and milk, in that order, and blend until smooth.

2. Pour into two glasses and serve.

 DID YOU KNOW? This smoothie gives you more than a quarter of the recommended daily calcium intake. Milk and almonds both have calcium, and that helps keep your bones and teeth strong. More sources of calcium include cheese, yogurt, kale, and broccoli.

Per serving: Calories: 436; Protein: 14g; Total carbs: 67g; Sugars: 45g; Fiber: 11g; Total fat: 16g; Saturated fat: 4g; Cholesterol: 20mg; Sodium: 118mg

Fruit and Honey Yogurt Parfait

Serves 2 • Prep time: 5 minutes

FEW INGREDIENTS • GLUTEN-FREE • UNDER 30 MINUTES • VEGETARIAN

If you're looking for a breakfast to fill you up, look no further than Greek yogurt. You'll notice that this recipe calls for whole-milk yogurt. Many studies have shown that full-fat yogurt is actually more helpful for weight loss than nonfat because it keeps you satisfied. As long as you are paying attention to your portion sizes, don't worry about the calorie difference.

1½ cups plain full-fat Greek yogurt

1½ cups mixed berries, such as blueberries, raspberries, or blackberries

2 tablespoons chopped walnuts

1 tablespoon honey

Pinch ground cinnamon

1. Divide ½ cup of the yogurt between two small bowls.

2. Add ¼ cup of berries on top of the yogurt.

3. Repeat this twice more, then top with the walnuts, honey, and cinnamon. Serve.

❖ **DID YOU KNOW?** Raspberries are high in fiber. One-half cup of raspberries gives you 4 grams of fiber. That's 16 percent of the daily recommended amount of fiber for women and 11 percent for men. You can use fresh or frozen berries in this recipe and get the same nutritional benefits.

Per serving: Calories: 288; Protein: 18g; Total carbs: 28g; Sugars: 23g; Fiber: 3g; Total fat: 12g; Saturated fat: 5g; Cholesterol: 28mg; Sodium: 81mg

Fruit and Nut Breakfast Bites

Serves 4 ◆ Prep time: 15 minutes

DAIRY-FREE ◆ FEW INGREDIENTS ◆ GLUTEN-FREE ◆ UNDER 30 MINUTES ◆ VEGAN

I like to keep energy bites around for busy days when I need a little something sweet but also want it to be healthy. Even a small serving of dried fruits and nuts satisfies quickly because of the high fiber content. These bites are great to keep in the refrigerator for those busy mornings when you need to just grab and go. You can also pair them with plain Greek yogurt to add more protein to your breakfast.

1 cup unsalted almonds

1 cup pitted dried dates

⅓ cup unsweetened dried cranberries

2 tablespoons gluten-free old-fashioned rolled oats

1. In a high-speed blender, place the almonds and process until they're the size of coarse breadcrumbs. Add the dates, cranberries, and oats and pulse until a smooth mixture forms. You may need to scrape down the sides a few times.

2. Scoop out a heaping tablespoon and form into a ball. Repeat to form 16 bites.

 VARIATION: There are many ways you can add variety to these breakfast bites. Keep the dates-to-oats ratio the same, and swap out the other ingredients for equal amounts of other nuts and dried fruit. Use cashews instead of almonds, for example, or substitute apricots for the cranberries.

Per serving (4 bites): Calories: 308; Protein: 7g; Total carbs: 41g; Sugars: 30g; Fiber: 7g; Total fat: 15g; Saturated fat: 1g; Cholesterol: 0mg; Sodium: 8mg

Crostini and Berry Plate with Feta-Ricotta Spread

Serves 2 ◆ Prep time: 10 minutes ◆ Cook time: 5 minutes
UNDER 30 MINUTES ◆ VEGETARIAN

I made this for my family one night as an accompaniment to dinner, and they raved about how it would make a perfect breakfast. I agree completely. It takes almost no time to prepare, and has all the makings of a perfect European breakfast: whole-grain bread, cheese, and fruit.

2 slices hearty
  whole-wheat bread

½ tablespoon extra-virgin
  olive oil

2 ounces crumbled
  feta cheese

2 tablespoons ricotta cheese

1 teaspoon honey

1 cup raspberries

1 cup blueberries

1 cup grapes

1. Preheat the oven to broil and line a baking sheet with aluminum foil.

2. Place the bread slices on the prepared baking sheet and brush with the oil. Broil for 2 to 3 minutes, until they are just starting to get golden brown.

3. Remove from the oven and cut each slice in half.

4. In a small bowl, combine the feta, ricotta, and honey, mixing until smooth and well incorporated. Spread the cheese mixture on the bread.

5. Divide the fruits into two servings and serve with the bread and cheese on the side.

 VARIATION: If you want to add more fruit to this dish, spread the feta-ricotta spread on apple slices instead of bread. Cut an apple into full circles and use a small paring knife to remove the core. Top each apple slice with some cheese spread.

Per serving: Calories: 360; Protein: 11g; Total carbs: 59g; Sugars: 31g; Fiber: 12g; Total fat: 12g; Saturated fat: 4g; Cholesterol: 24mg; Sodium: 414mg

Grab-and-Go Breakfast Pack

Serves 2 ◆ Prep time: 5 minutes ◆ Cook time: 15 minutes

FEW INGREDIENTS ◆ GLUTEN-FREE ◆ ONE POT ◆ UNDER 30 MINUTES ◆ VEGETARIAN

You might see grab-and-go packs at your local coffee shop or deli, but you probably don't feel like overspending on something you could make at home. That's good thinking. You need a few things to make your breakfast a hit and keep you fueled up: protein, fiber, and complex carbs. Use containers that have separate compartments, if you have them, to keep everything fresh and ready for multiple mornings.

2 large eggs

1 cup blueberries

30 unsalted almonds

2 ounces whole-milk mozzarella cheese, cut into cubes

1. In a medium saucepan over high heat, add the eggs and enough cold water to cover them and bring to a boil. Boil for 4 minutes, then turn off the heat and let the eggs sit for 10 minutes. Transfer them to cool water and peel.

2. In each of two separate containers place: 1 peeled hardboiled egg, ½ cup of blueberries, 15 almonds, and 1 ounce of mozzarella cheese.

 COOKING TIP: You can make the hardboiled eggs on Sunday and grab one every day for breakfast. These packs can be assembled in advance or made quickly in the morning—perfect for the entire family.

Per serving: Calories: 308; Protein: 16g; Total carbs: 16g; Sugars: 9g; Fiber: 4g; Total fat: 21g; Saturated fat: 7g; Cholesterol: 189mg; Sodium: 257mg

Make-Ahead Muesli

Serves 6 ◆ Prep time: 5 minutes ◆ Cook time: 45 minutes

DAIRY-FREE ◆ FEW INGREDIENTS ◆ GLUTEN-FREE ◆ VEGETARIAN

The muesli you'll find in any grocery store in Europe is like an American version of granola. My favorite European muesli has baked oats, almonds, and freeze-dried strawberries—and it's perfect for snacking, too. Eat it alone or with milk and fresh berries. Using freeze-dried fruit helps keep the sugar low. This is basic muesli, so you can add other flavors to make it your own. If you have unsweetened coconut or raisins, add them when you add the strawberries. You can also stir in ¼ cup of nut butter before baking for an extra protein kick.

3 cups gluten-free old-fashioned rolled oats

¼ cup canola oil

¼ cup honey

¼ teaspoon kosher salt

½ cup sliced or slivered unsalted almonds

1 cup freeze-dried strawberries

1. Preheat the oven to 300°F. Line a baking sheet with parchment paper.

2. In a large bowl, combine the oats, oil, honey, and salt and mix together well. Spread the mixture evenly on the prepared baking sheet and bake for 30 minutes, stirring every 15 minutes. Add the almonds to the baking sheet, stir, and bake for 15 more minutes.

3. Remove the baking sheet from the oven and leave the muesli at room temperature to crisp up (it will still look and feel moist).

4. When it is completely cool, transfer it to an airtight container and add the freeze-dried fruit.

 COOKING TIP: Always use the type of salt specified in the recipe. Table salt has smaller and finer crystals than kosher salt, so that means there's more salt in 1 teaspoon of table salt than there is in 1 teaspoon of kosher salt. In other words, if you're out of kosher salt and you use table salt instead, one for one, your food will be too salty. That also means you'll get more sodium—not good if you're watching your blood pressure.

Per serving: Calories: 341; Protein: 7g; Total carbs: 44g; Sugars: 14g; Fiber: 6g; Total fat: 16g; Saturated fat: 2g; Cholesterol: 0mg; Sodium: 101mg

Porridge with Blueberries

Serves 2 ◆ Prep time: 5 minutes ◆ Cook time: 25 minutes

FEW INGREDIENTS ◆ GLUTEN-FREE ◆ ONE POT ◆ UNDER 30 MINUTES ◆ VEGETARIAN

If you need a breakfast to really fill you up, this is it. Steel-cut oats take a little longer to cook, but they are so worth it. They have a nutty, chewy texture that makes a creamy porridge which is both hearty and satisfying. You can use any type of berry you choose—or fruit for that matter—to add fiber and sweetness to your porridge.

½ cup gluten-free
steel-cut oats

1½ cups 2% milk

2 teaspoons honey

½ teaspoon
ground cinnamon

1 cup blueberries

1. In a small saucepan over medium-low heat, add the oats, milk, honey, and cinnamon. Bring the mixture to a light simmer and cook, stirring every 3 to 4 minutes, for 20 to 25 minutes, until the oats are soft with just a little "bite." The porridge will get creamier as you stir.

2. For each serving, put ¼ cup of blueberries in a bowl, top with half of the porridge, and add another ¼ cup of berries on top.

 DID YOU KNOW? There are many different types of oats in the grocery store. They are all good for you, so which one you choose really depends on how much time you have. Steel-cut oats are cut into pieces; old-fashioned rolled oats are thinner and absorb water faster. Instant and quick-cook oats are thinner and chopped small to absorb water faster still.

Per serving: Calories: 308; Protein: 12g; Total carbs: 53g; Sugars: 23g; Fiber: 6g; Total fat: 7g; Saturated fat: 3g; Cholesterol: 15mg; Sodium: 90mg

Smoked Salmon and Avocado Toast

Serves 2 ◆ Prep time: 5 minutes ◆ Cook time: 5 minutes

DAIRY-FREE ◆ FEW INGREDIENTS ◆ ONE PAN ◆ UNDER 30 MINUTES

I have two daughters who like to start the day on a healthier note than with sugary cereals that might as well be dessert. My youngest tells me she could eat avocado toast for every meal, and my oldest daughter's favorite breakfast is smoked salmon with cream cheese on toast. I decided to combine the two, and it was a huge hit in my home. I hope it is in yours, too.

2 slices hearty
   whole-wheat bread

1 teaspoon extra-virgin
   olive oil

⅛ teaspoon kosher salt

⅛ teaspoon black pepper

½ avocado, thinly sliced

4 ounces smoked salmon

1. Preheat the oven to broil. Line a baking sheet with aluminum foil.

2. Place the bread on the prepared baking sheet. Brush with the oil and sprinkle with the salt and black pepper. Broil for 1 to 2 minutes, just until the bread starts to brown.

3. Divide the avocado slices between the toast and smash down lightly with a fork.

4. Place the salmon on top and serve immediately.

 SUBSTITUTION TIP: If smoked salmon is not available or you just don't like it, try this with very thinly sliced smoked ham. Even though ham is a processed meat, having it every once in a while will not harm your health or prevent weight loss.

Per serving: Calories: 263; Protein: 16g; Total carbs: 25g; Sugars: 5g; Fiber: 7g; Total fat: 12g; Saturated fat: 2g; Cholesterol: 13mg; Sodium: 634mg

Caprese Breakfast Sandwich

Serves 2 ◆ Prep time: 5 minutes ◆ Cook time: 5 minutes

FEW INGREDIENTS ◆ ONE PAN ◆ UNDER 30 MINUTES ◆ VEGETARIAN

With all the good food in France, you might not guess it, but my favorite food to grab on the go is a tomato and mozzarella baguette. It's portable, delicious, and fills me up. It's also my preferred way to get my calcium. I modified this sandwich just a little to make it easier for you in the morning. Baguettes go stale quickly and don't give you much fiber, so try this with a whole-wheat English muffin.

2 whole-wheat English muffins

2 tablespoons basil pesto

2 (1-ounce) slices mozzarella cheese

1 large tomato, cut into ¼-inch-thick slices

10 baby spinach leaves

1. Preheat the oven to broil. Line a baking sheet with aluminum foil.

2. Halve the English muffins and arrange then on the prepared baking sheet. Spread ½ tablespoon of pesto on each half, then top each with a slice of mozzarella.

3. Place under the broiler for about 1 minute, until the cheese is just melted.

4. Add the tomato slices and spinach to each sandwich, and serve.

 DID YOU KNOW? Fresh mozzarella is high in calcium and protein. Choose the mozzarella you can slice yourself. You can use any leftover cheese in the Grab-and-Go Breakfast Pack (page 64) or save it to put in your Antipasto Salad (page 95).

Per serving: Calories: 304; Protein: 15g; Total carbs: 33g; Sugars: 8g; Fiber: 7g; Total fat: 14g; Saturated fat: 6g; Cholesterol: 25mg; Sodium: 643mg

Spanakopita Breakfast Pitas

Serves 2 ◆ Prep time: 5 minutes ◆ Cook time: 5 minutes

FEW INGREDIENTS ◆ UNDER 30 MINUTES ◆ VEGETARIAN

It's possible to have a hot breakfast that doesn't take all morning to bake. I love to start getting my veggies early in the day, because it makes me feel like I've accomplished a goal early. I hope it does the same for you.

2 whole-wheat pita rounds

½ cup packed baby spinach leaves

2 large eggs

Nonstick cooking spray

2 ounces crumbled feta cheese

1. Halve the pita rounds across the middle and stuff each half with five or six spinach leaves.

2. In a small bowl, whisk the eggs.

3. Spray a small nonstick skillet with cooking spray and place over medium heat. Add the eggs and the feta. Move the eggs around with a spatula for 2 to 3 minutes, until they are just cooked.

4. Divide the egg mixture evenly between the four pita halves and serve.

 DID YOU KNOW? Spanakopita is a traditional Greek dish made with layers of phyllo dough and filled with spinach and feta cheese. Since it has "pita" in the name, I decided to turn this into a breakfast dish with the same flavors.

Per serving: Calories: 244; Protein: 13g; Total carbs: 33g; Sugars: 3g; Fiber: 4g; Total fat: 8g; Saturated fat: 3g; Cholesterol: 173mg; Sodium: 407mg

Mediterranean Eggs Breakfast Sandwich

Serves 2 ◆ Prep time: 5 minutes ◆ Cook time: 10 minutes

FEW INGREDIENTS ◆ UNDER 30 MINUTES ◆ VEGETARIAN

Getting enough fiber and protein at breakfast is essential to keeping hunger away through the morning hours. A sandwich is in no way a typical Mediterranean breakfast, but taking a few popular ingredients from the region and weaving them into a familiar dish will have you mastering Mediterranean cooking in no time.

2 whole-wheat English muffins

2 large eggs

2 ounces crumbled feta cheese

Nonstick cooking spray

6 cherry tomatoes, chopped

2 cups packed baby spinach

1. Toast the English muffins.

2. In a small bowl, whisk the eggs, then add the feta.

3. Spray a small nonstick skillet with cooking spray and place over medium heat. Add the tomatoes and spinach. Cook, stirring, for 2 to 3 minutes, until the spinach starts to wilt.

4. Add the egg mixture directly over the tomatoes and spinach, and let them cook without disturbing them for 3 to 4 minutes, until the bottom has set. Flip the eggs over, then fold them in half.

5. Divide the eggs in half, assemble the two sandwiches, and serve.

 VARIATION: If you have leftover roasted vegetables, those can be chopped small and used instead of the tomatoes and spinach. Adding roasted vegetables to your breakfast gets you on the fast track to getting enough vegetables into your day.

Per serving: Calories: 243; Protein: 14g; Total carbs: 31g; Sugars: 8g; Fiber: 6g; Total fat: 8g; Saturated fat: 3g; Cholesterol: 173mg; Sodium: 428mg

Spanish-Style Scrambled Eggs

Serves 2 ◆ Prep time: 5 minutes ◆ Cook time: 10 minutes

DAIRY-FREE ◆ GLUTEN-FREE ◆ UNDER 30 MINUTES ◆ VEGETARIAN

Adding herbs and spices can perk up your scrambled eggs in the morning; they are common in Europe, as are vegetables with breakfast. (Snack peppers are mini bell peppers—they're colorful and naturally sweet.) The small amount of smoked paprika in these eggs is not overpowering, but is undeniably Spanish. If you have some Manchego cheese in your refrigerator, grate a little over the top for extra Spanish flair.

½ tablespoon extra-virgin olive oil

10 cherry tomatoes

4 snack peppers, halved and seeded

1 scallion, white and green parts, thinly sliced, divided

4 large eggs

¼ teaspoon kosher salt

¼ teaspoon ground cumin

⅛ teaspoon smoked paprika

1. In a small skillet over medium heat, combine the oil, tomatoes, peppers, and the white parts of the scallion. Sauté for about 4 minutes, until the tomatoes start to burst. Remove the vegetables from skillet and divide into two serving bowls.

2. In a medium bowl, whisk together the eggs, salt, cumin, and paprika to combine. Add the egg mixture to the hot skillet and cook, moving around with a spatula, for about 3 minutes, until the eggs are cooked through. Add the scrambled eggs to each bowl with the vegetables.

3. Garnish with the green parts of the scallion and serve.

 DID YOU KNOW? Eggs are still a hot topic in the nutrition world. An important source of high-quality protein, choline, and vitamin B_{12}, they are also high in cholesterol. While there is no consensus on the egg's role in blood cholesterol levels, it's best to limit your intake of egg yolks to no more than three per week. If you have high cholesterol, make this dish with one whole egg plus one egg white.

Per serving: Calories: 202; Protein: 13g; Total carbs: 8g; Sugars: 6g; Fiber: 2g; Total fat: 13g; Saturated fat: 3g; Cholesterol: 328mg; Sodium: 255mg

Sun-Dried Tomato and Spinach Frittata

Serves 4 • Prep time: 5 minutes • Cook time: 20 minutes

FEW INGREDIENTS • GLUTEN-FREE • UNDER 30 MINUTES • VEGETARIAN

This thin frittata cooks fast and has so much flavor, you might not believe each serving is under 100 calories. This gives you room to add a slice of whole-wheat toast or a big bowl of fruit to round out your breakfast. Store the extra slices in the refrigerator. Leftover frittata makes a yummy breakfast sandwich.

Nonstick cooking spray

4 large eggs

¼ cup 2% milk

½ teaspoon kosher salt

¼ teaspoon black pepper

1 cup packed baby spinach

2 tablespoons chopped
sun-dried tomatoes

1. Preheat the oven to 350°F. Spray a 9-inch oven-safe skillet or well-seasoned cast-iron skillet with cooking spray.

2. In a medium bowl, whisk together the eggs, milk, salt, and black pepper. Add the spinach and mix.

3. Pour the mixture into the skillet and place the sun-dried tomatoes on top, making sure they are evenly dispersed. Bake for 20 minutes, or until the center is no longer runny.

4. Remove the skillet from the oven and let it rest for 5 minutes before serving.

 COOKING TIP: If you don't have an oven-safe skillet, you could make this in a baking dish of the same size. You could also make these in mini muffin cups; just watch the time because your eggs will cook faster.

Per serving: Calories: 84; Protein: 7g; Total carbs: 3g; Sugars: 2g; Fiber: <1g; Total fat: 5g; Saturated fat: 2g; Cholesterol: 166mg; Sodium: 209mg

CHAPTER 6

Snacks

◇◇◇◇◇◇◇◇◇◇◇◇◇◇◇◇◇◇

Marinated Olives with Herbs and Lemon

Serves 4 ◆ Prep time: 5 minutes

DAIRY-FREE ◆ FEW INGREDIENTS ◆ GLUTEN-FREE ◆ UNDER 30 MINUTES ◆ VEGAN

Mediterranean eating would not be complete without olives. They are the perfect choice for a quick snack. They are brined, so they add a little sodium to your diet. Make sure you keep your serving size to about 10 small olives or 5 big ones. The lemon peel in this dish is edible as long as you use just the yellow part and leave out the bitter white part. Lemon peel has antioxidants and tastes delicious with olives.

1 small lemon

40 small olives, a variety of black, green, and Kalamata olives

2 teaspoons extra-virgin olive oil

½ teaspoon Italian seasoning

1. Thoroughly wash and dry the lemon. Using a vegetable peeler, peel off slices of the yellow part of the rind. Put the lemon in a small container to save for another dish.

2. Place the rind in a small bowl. Add the olives, oil, and Italian seasoning, mixing to combine. Store in the refrigerator or portion out for snacks.

 DID YOU KNOW? Most of the olives grown around the Mediterranean are used for olive oil. When we visited Naples, the house we stayed in was surrounded by the most beautiful olive trees, but alas, none to eat. They must be brined before they can be eaten.

Per serving: Calories: 62; Protein: <1g; Total carbs: 3g; Sugars: <1g; Fiber: 1g; Total fat: 6g; Saturated fat: 1g; Cholesterol: 0mg; Sodium: 236mg

Rosemary Roasted Almonds

Serves 4 • Prep time: 5 minutes • Cook time: 10 minutes

DAIRY-FREE • FEW INGREDIENTS • GLUTEN-FREE • ONE PAN • UNDER 30 MINUTES • VEGAN

I think I ate my weight in Marcona almonds while in Spain. They have a rich, buttery texture and are so good. They are more widely available in the United States now and are worth trying at least once. Some nuts can have a bitter taste, but Marcona almonds are mild and might become your favorite, too.

1 cup unsalted
 Marcona almonds

2 teaspoons extra-virgin
 olive oil

1 teaspoon chopped
 fresh rosemary

¼ teaspoon sea salt

1. Preheat the oven to 350°F. Line a baking sheet with parchment paper.

2. Place the almonds on the prepared baking sheet, drizzle them with the oil, and sprinkle the rosemary and the salt on top. Toss to coat, then shake the pan so the almonds are evenly spread out.

3. Roast for 10 minutes, until the almonds are just lightly golden.

4. Remove from the oven, let the almonds cool on the baking sheet, then store them in an airtight container or portion out into individual servings.

 SUBSTITUTION TIP: If you can't find these almonds, any type of unsalted almond—or nut for that matter—would work in this recipe.

Per serving: Calories: 220; Protein: 7g; Total carbs: 6g; Sugars: 2g; Fiber: 3g; Total fat: 20g; Saturated fat: 2g; Cholesterol: 0mg; Sodium: 151mg

Parmesan and Herb Popcorn

Serves 4 • Prep time: 5 minutes • Cook time: 10 minutes

FEW INGREDIENTS • GLUTEN-FREE • ONE POT • UNDER 30 MINUTES • VEGETARIAN

Popcorn is my snack of choice. My son feels the same way, and asks for it at least three times a week. We like to try out different spice and herb combinations to see which ones we like best. It's a challenge for me to see how fast I can get the Parmesan cheese on the hot popcorn so that it melts nicely.

1 tablespoon canola oil

½ cup popcorn kernels

¼ cup freshly grated
   Parmesan cheese

¼ teaspoon kosher salt

¼ teaspoon Italian seasoning

1. Heat a medium pot, Dutch oven, or deep skillet over medium-high heat. Add the oil, cover, and heat for 3 minutes.

2. Add the popcorn, close the lid, and wait for the popping to start. When it does, carefully shake the pot every minute until you hear the popping slow or stop.

3. Remove the pot from the heat, pour the popcorn into a large bowl, and immediately add the Parmesan cheese and toss. Add the salt and Italian seasoning and toss again. Serve.

 COOKING TIP: If you have an air popper, use that and skip the oil.

Per serving: Calories: 167; Protein: 5g; Total carbs: 23g; Sugars: 0g; Fiber: 4g; Total fat: 7g; Saturated fat: 1g; Cholesterol: 5mg; Sodium: 260mg

Spiced Crunchy Chickpeas

Serves 2 ◆ Prep time: 10 minutes ◆ Cook time: 40 minutes

DAIRY-FREE ◆ GLUTEN-FREE ◆ ONE PAN ◆ VEGAN

Crunchy chickpeas are my new favorite snack. It's a snack that changes its form with whatever you have in your spice cabinet. I usually have to double the recipe when I make these because my kids eat them like candy.

1 (15-ounce) can chickpeas, drained and rinsed

1 tablespoon extra-virgin olive oil

½ teaspoon ground cumin

½ teaspoon paprika

½ teaspoon ground coriander

¼ teaspoon garlic powder

¼ teaspoon kosher salt

½ teaspoon dried parsley

1. Preheat the oven to 400°F. Line a baking sheet with aluminum foil.

2. Spread the chickpeas on a clean towel and dry them thoroughly. Remove and discard the skins from each chickpea by slightly pinching each; the skin will slide off.

3. Place the chickpeas on the baking sheet, drizzle them with the oil, and season them with the cumin, paprika, coriander, garlic powder, and salt. Shake the pan to coat the chickpeas in the oil and spices.

4. Bake for 40 minutes, gently giving the pan a shake halfway through, until the chickpeas turn dark and golden and easily roll around on the pan.

5. Remove from the oven and sprinkle the parsley on top. Cool before eating.

 COOKING TIP: There are a couple of tricks to making crunchy chickpeas. The first is to remove the skins. Moisture can get trapped under the skins and that will make it difficult for the chickpeas to get crunchy. The second is to let them cool completely before putting them in a container. Any heat left on the chickpeas will create moisture in a sealed container, and they will not stay crispy for long.

Per serving: Calories: 250; Protein: 10g; Total carbs: 31g; Sugars: 5g; Fiber: 9g; Total fat: 11g; Saturated fat: 1g; Cholesterol: 0mg; Sodium: 579mg

Cucumber, Cheese, and Spinach Roll-Ups

Serves 4 • Prep time: 10 minutes

FEW INGREDIENTS • GLUTEN-FREE • UNDER 30 MINUTES • VEGETARIAN

These are meant to be a snack, but also double as a fun appetizer for lunch or dinner. By adding a sensible portion of cream cheese, you bring out the flavors of the cucumbers and spinach, and it definitely makes eating your vegetables more interesting. If you have cucumber left over from this, save it to use in Fattoush (page 94) or Crudités with Tzatziki (page 85). Use a mandoline, if you have one, or a very sharp knife to cut the cucumber into long, thin ribbons.

1 English cucumber

8 teaspoons chive cream cheese

40 baby spinach leaves

1. Cut the cucumber lengthwise into eight long ribbons, each about 1/16-inch thick.

2. Leaving a half inch at the end of the cucumber ribbon, spread five spinach leaves and 1 teaspoon of cream cheese, then roll up the ribbon. Secure with a toothpick if desired. Repeat to make all of the roll-ups.

 DID YOU KNOW? These fun snacks are a hit with kids. If your little one wants to help out in the kitchen, have them count out the spinach leaves for each roll.

Per serving (2 rolls): Calories: 60; Protein: 4g; Total carbs: 6g; Sugars: 2g; Fiber: 3g; Total fat: 3g; Saturated fat: 2g; Cholesterol: 8mg; Sodium: 135mg

Watermelon Sticks with Cinnamon Honey Yogurt

Serves 4 ◆ Prep time: 10 minutes

FEW INGREDIENTS ◆ GLUTEN-FREE ◆ UNDER 30 MINUTES ◆ VEGETARIAN

The Mediterranean diet is not only packed with vegetables, but it also places a large emphasis on fruit. Watermelon is a popular fruit in the countries that surround the Mediterranean Sea and was even a favorite in ancient Egypt. This dip works with any melon that is in season. And if melon is not in season, cutting an apple into sticks is a fun way to enjoy it all year round.

1 cup plain full-fat
  Greek yogurt

1 tablespoon honey

1 teaspoon ground cinnamon

1 small seedless watermelon,
  cut into ½-inch sticks

1. In a small serving bowl, mix together the yogurt, honey, and cinnamon.

2. Serve with the watermelon for dipping.

 COOKING TIP: To make watermelon sticks, cut off the rind on the stem end and use it as a flat, steady base. Then continue to cut off the rind until you are left with just watermelon flesh. Cut the flesh in half and keep cutting in half until you get ½-inch sticks, then cut to the length you want.

Per serving: Calories: 121; Protein: 7g; Total carbs: 20g; Sugars: 17g; Fiber: 1g; Total fat: 3g; Saturated fat: 2g; Cholesterol: 9mg; Sodium: 25mg

Pistachio and Cranberry Snack Bars

Makes 9 bars ◆ Prep time: 10 minutes ◆ Cook time: 25 minutes

DAIRY-FREE ◆ GLUTEN-FREE ◆ VEGETARIAN

Stocking up on "health bars" at the store can get expensive and doesn't help you avoid ultraprocessed foods. These snack bars are perfect for that sweet and chocolaty craving, and they won't leave you feeling like you need to cut back somewhere else. There are several ingredients, but you just add them all to one bowl, stir, and transfer to a baking dish—and you're done.

1 cup gluten-free old-fashioned rolled oats

¼ cup coconut oil

¼ cup almond butter

¼ cup honey

2 tablespoons unsweetened cocoa powder

1 large egg

1 teaspoon vanilla extract

½ teaspoon ground cinnamon

¼ teaspoon kosher salt

½ cup chopped unsalted pistachios

½ cup unsweetened dried cranberries

1. Preheat the oven to 350°F. Line an 8-by-8-inch baking dish with parchment paper.

2. Divide up your oats: Put ½ cup in a large bowl and set aside. Put the remaining ½ cup in a blender and blend into oat flour. Add the oat flour to the bowl.

3. Add the oil, almond butter, honey, cocoa powder, egg, vanilla, cinnamon, salt, pistachios, and cranberries and stir well. Transfer the mixture to the prepared baking dish and spread out evenly.

4. Bake for 22 to 25 minutes, or until a toothpick inserted into the center comes out clean.

5. Let cool completely before cutting into nine bars. Store them in an airtight container at room temperature for up to three days.

 SUBSTITUTION TIP: You can substitute any nut butters or any nuts if almond butter or pistachios are not your favorite.

Per serving (1 bar): Calories: 232; Protein: 5g; Total carbs: 23g; Sugars: 14g; Fiber: 3g; Total fat: 14g; Saturated fat: 6g; Cholesterol: 21mg; Sodium: 80mg

Tomato and Scallion Bruschetta

Serves 2 ◆ Prep time: 5 minutes ◆ Cook time: 5 minutes

DAIRY-FREE ◆ FEW INGREDIENTS ◆ UNDER 30 MINUTES ◆ VEGAN

Years ago, I spent three months in Sicily, and every time I went out to eat, I ordered bruschetta. It's a little different everywhere you go, but my favorite was fresh tomatoes with olive oil and thin slices of scallion on toasted baguette. It's a dish I crave now and eat often as an appetizer or snack. This is a true Italian favorite.

8 slices small baguette

2 tablespoons extra-virgin olive oil, divided

2 Roma tomatoes, chopped

1 scallion, white and green parts, finely sliced

¼ teaspoon kosher salt

⅛ teaspoon black pepper

1. Preheat the oven to broil. Line a baking sheet with aluminum foil.

2. Arrange the baguette slices on the prepared baking sheet and brush with 1 tablespoon of oil. Broil for 2 to 3 minutes, until the baguette slices just start to brown.

3. In a small bowl, combine the tomatoes, scallion, remaining 1 tablespoon of oil, salt, and black pepper. Gently toss to mix.

4. To assemble the bruschetta, spoon some tomato mixture on top of the bread. Serve immediately.

 VARIATION: If you can't find a small baguette, try slicing up a zucchini and use it instead of bread. You can broil it for the same amount of time to warm it up but keep the crunch.

Per serving: Calories: 432; Protein: 11g; Total carbs: 67g; Sugars: 2g; Fiber: 1g; Total fat: 14g; Saturated fat: 2g; Cholesterol: 0mg; Sodium: 1,059mg

Roasted Garlic Hummus

Serves 6 ♦ Prep time: 10 minutes ♦ Cook time: 30 minutes

DAIRY-FREE ♦ GLUTEN-FREE ♦ VEGAN

Hummus is a traditional Middle Eastern dip that has been adopted and adapted in many countries. It's typically made from chickpeas and tahini, which is sesame seed paste. Tahini is turning up at more and more supermarkets, and you can always find it in a health food store or online. Hummus is the perfect vessel for the flavors of the Mediterranean, including roasted garlic.

1 whole head garlic, unpeeled

1 (15-ounce) can chickpeas, drained and rinsed

2 tablespoons tahini

1 tablespoon freshly squeezed lemon juice

½ teaspoon kosher salt

½ teaspoon ground cumin

3 tablespoons extra-virgin olive oil

2 tablespoons water, as needed

1. Preheat the oven to 400°F.

2. Wrap the garlic in a piece of aluminum foil and roast it for 30 minutes. Unwrap and cool before using.

3. Cut the top of the garlic bulb off to expose the cloves. Squeeze all the cloves into a blender. Add the chickpeas, tahini, lemon juice, salt, cumin, and oil.

4. Pulse the ingredients until smooth. Add the water, a little at a time, if needed, until the consistency is smooth, like warm peanut butter.

 COOKING TIP: If you are using the oven for another dish earlier in the week, put this garlic in to roast. You can roast the garlic up to two days before you need it. Squeeze out the garlic into a small container and keep it in the refrigerator until you're ready to use it.

Per serving (¼ cup): Calories: 157; Protein: 4g; Total carbs: 12g; Sugars: 2g; Fiber: 3g; Total fat: 11g; Saturated fat: 1g; Cholesterol: 0mg; Sodium: 194mg

Crudités with Tzatziki

Serves 2 ◆ Prep time: 10 minutes

FEW INGREDIENTS ◆ GLUTEN-FREE ◆ UNDER 30 MINUTES ◆ VEGETARIAN

I like to call this tzatziki my all-purpose dip. I use it for everything: veggies, chicken, wraps, salads. It's so refreshing and comes together quick. You'll find it pairs well with many dishes in this book. I like to keep some in the refrigerator because I'm a dipper. I love my veggies, but I have to have some dip with them. Use your favorite vegetables to dip. Carrots, radishes, zucchini, and cucumbers all stand up well to dipping.

1 cucumber, divided

1 cup plain full-fat
Greek yogurt

1 teaspoon freshly squeezed
lemon juice

1 teaspoon chopped fresh dill,
or ½ teaspoon dried dill

¼ teaspoon kosher salt

2 large carrots, cut into sticks

1. Using the largest holes of a box grater, grate your cucumber until you have a little over ¼ cup. Place the grated cucumber in a clean dish towel or strong paper towel and squeeze out the liquid. Add the grated cucumber to a small bowl.

2. Cut the rest of the cucumber into slices and set aside.

3. To the bowl, add the yogurt, lemon juice, dill, and salt and stir.

4. Serve the dip with the carrot sticks and cucumber slices, or portion out for snacks.

 DID YOU KNOW? Research into full-fat versus low-fat dairy and obesity risk isn't clear. That doesn't mean you can eat full-fat with no discretion, but it does mean having full-fat dairy every once in a while isn't going to hurt your weight loss goals. Plus, it may help you feel more satisfied after you eat.

Per serving: Calories: 150; Protein: 12g; Total carbs: 15g; Sugars: 9g; Fiber: 3g; Total fat: 5g; Saturated fat: 3g; Cholesterol: 19mg; Sodium: 393mg

Crudités with Roasted Eggplant Spread

Serves 4 ◆ Prep time: 10 minutes ◆ Cook time: 25 minutes

GLUTEN-FREE ◆ ONE PAN ◆ VEGETARIAN

If you enjoy eggplant, you will crave this zesty spread. To bring some extra texture and flavor to this snack, I jazz it up with olives and feta. I like using cucumber or summer squash slices instead of bread to keep the calories low.

1 eggplant

4 teaspoons extra-virgin olive oil, divided

½ teaspoon kosher salt, divided

2 garlic cloves, peeled

1 tablespoon freshly squeezed lemon juice

4 green or Kalamata olives

2 tablespoons crumbled feta cheese

1 small cucumber, cut into slices

1 small summer squash, cut into slices

1. Preheat the oven to 400°F. Line a baking sheet with aluminum foil.

2. Halve the eggplant lengthwise and brush 1 teaspoon of oil over the flesh. Place it, flesh-side up, on the prepared baking sheet. Sprinkle ¼ teaspoon of salt over the top.

3. Wrap the garlic in a small piece of foil and place it on the baking sheet with the eggplant. Roast for 25 minutes, or until the eggplant flesh is lightly browned and soft.

4. Remove from the oven and let the eggplant rest until it's cool enough to handle, then scoop out the flesh into a small serving bowl. Add the garlic to the serving bowl and mash the eggplant and garlic together with a fork. Add the lemon juice, 2 teaspoons of oil, and the remaining ¼ teaspoon of salt and mix together.

5. Make a small well in the middle the eggplant mixture and add the remaining 1 teaspoon of oil and the olives. Sprinkle the feta on top.

6. Serve with the cucumber and summer squash for dipping.

 DID YOU KNOW? There are many types of eggplant, and they vary in both size and color. Choose an Italian or Sicilian eggplant for a dish like this to maximize the amount of flesh you get.

Per serving: Calories: 107; Protein: 3g; Total carbs: 12g; Sugars: 7g; Fiber: 5g; Total fat: 6g; Saturated fat: 1g; Cholesterol: 4mg; Sodium: 253mg

Ricotta Spinach Dip
with Carrot Sticks

Serves 4 ◆ Prep time: 10 minutes ◆ Cook time: 15 minutes

GLUTEN-FREE ◆ ONE PAN ◆ UNDER 30 MINUTES ◆ VEGETARIAN

This fresh and zesty dip is taken to the next level with the addition of chive cream cheese. You can use any leftover cream cheese for the Cucumber, Cheese, and Spinach Roll-Ups (page 80).

1 tablespoon extra-virgin olive oil

1 small onion, chopped

1 garlic clove, minced

2 cups chopped baby spinach

6 ounces ricotta cheese

2 ounces chive cream cheese

¼ cup freshly grated Parmesan cheese

4 large carrots, cut into sticks

1. Preheat the oven to 400°F.

2. In a small oven-proof skillet over medium heat, add the oil, onions, garlic, and spinach and sauté, stirring continuously, for 2 to 3 minutes, until the spinach is wilted. Turn off the heat and add the ricotta cheese, cream cheese, and Parmesan cheese, stirring throughout.

3. Bake for 10 minutes, or until the top is browned.

4. Serve with the carrots.

 COOKING TIP: If you don't have an oven-proof skillet, transfer the mixture to a small baking dish to bake your dip.

Per serving: Calories: 198; Protein: 7g; Total carbs: 14g; Sugars: 6g; Fiber: 3g; Total fat: 13g; Saturated fat: 6g; Cholesterol: 35mg; Sodium: 291mg

CHAPTER 7

Salads and Soups

◇◇◇◇◇◇◇◇◇◇◇◇◇◇◇◇◇◇◇◇◇◇◇◇◇◇◇◇◇◇◇◇◇◇◇◇◇◇

Weeknight Garden Salad with Vinaigrette

Serves 2 • Prep time: 10 minutes

DAIRY-FREE • GLUTEN-FREE • UNDER 30 MINUTES • VEGAN

I always try to have at least one salad a day because it's a great way to eat a lot of vegetables at once. For most of the dinners in this book, there is time to fix a quick salad like this while the main dish is cooking. In the variation tip, I've provided some options for the vinaigrette so you can change things up from week to week.

FOR THE SALAD

1 (10-ounce) bag
  mixed greens

1 large tomato, chopped

1 small cucumber, chopped

1 small red onion,
  thinly sliced

FOR THE VINAIGRETTE

2 tablespoons extra-virgin
  olive oil

1 teaspoon Dijon mustard

¼ teaspoon kosher salt

⅛ teaspoon black pepper

1 tablespoon white
  wine vinegar

1 teaspoon sugar

½ teaspoon Italian seasoning

TO MAKE THE SALAD

1. Combine the greens, tomato, cucumber, and onion in a medium serving bowl.

TO MAKE THE VINAIGRETTE

2. Combine the oil, mustard, salt, black pepper, vinegar, sugar, and Italian seasoning in a small covered container and shake to mix.

3. Drizzle the dressing over the salad, toss to combine, and serve.

 VARIATION: I like to change up the dressing on this salad to keep things interesting. To turn it into a balsamic vinaigrette, replace the white wine vinegar, sugar, and Italian seasoning with 2 tablespoons of balsamic vinegar. To make a lemon vinaigrette, leave out the same ingredients and add 1 tablespoon of lemon juice and 1 tablespoon of water.

Per serving: Calories: 210; Protein: 4g; Total carbs: 19g; Sugars: 9g; Fiber: 6g; Total fat: 14g; Saturated fat: 2g; Cholesterol: 0mg; Sodium: 396mg

Classic Greek Salad

Serves 4 ♦ Prep time: 10 minutes

GLUTEN-FREE ♦ UNDER 30 MINUTES ♦ VEGETARIAN

You can't start a Mediterranean lifestyle and not have a recipe for Greek salad. At the heart of it is the freshness that is symbolic of the region's cuisine. There are many variations that include extras like greens and even fruit, but a Greek salad's hallmark ingredients are cucumber, tomatoes, red onion, feta cheese, and olives, dressed with heart-healthy olive oil.

4 vine-ripened tomatoes, cut into bite-size pieces

½ teaspoon kosher salt, divided

1 English cucumber, cut into bite-size pieces

1 green bell pepper, thinly sliced

1 small red onion, thinly sliced

20 Kalamata olives

12 green olives

1 (4-ounce) block feta cheese

2 tablespoons extra-virgin olive oil

½ teaspoon dried oregano

¼ teaspoon black pepper

1. Place the tomatoes in a large serving bowl. Sprinkle with ¼ teaspoon of salt and toss together.

2. Add the cucumber, bell pepper, onion, Kalamata olives, and green olives and toss gently. Place the feta on the top.

3. Drizzle the oil over the salad and sprinkle with the remaining ¼ teaspoon of salt. Add the oregano and black pepper and serve.

❖ **DID YOU KNOW?** Around the Mediterranean, when feta cheese is part of the dish, it is not crumbled; the entire block is placed on top for diners to break up as they eat. Look for a block that is only ½-inch thick to stay true to this salad.

Per serving: Calories: 263; Protein: 6g; Total carbs: 15g; Sugars: 7g; Fiber: 3g; Total fat: 21g; Saturated fat: 5g; Cholesterol: 25mg; Sodium: 1032mg

Lemon Chickpea Salad on Arugula

Serves 4 ◆ Prep time: 10 minutes

DAIRY-FREE ◆ GLUTEN-FREE ◆ UNDER 30 MINUTES ◆ VEGAN

This quick salad is easy to pull together as a side dish for dinner while your main dish is cooking. Lemons are a favorite citrus fruit in Italy and are used in sweet and savory dishes alike. If you're packing this up for a lunch on the go, pack the chickpeas separately from the arugula until you're ready to eat; this will keep your greens fresh and crisp.

1 (15-ounce) can chickpeas, drained and rinsed

1 small shallot, minced

Zest and juice of 1 lemon

2 tablespoons extra-virgin olive oil

1 tablespoon minced fresh chives

1 tablespoon minced fresh basil

1 tablespoon minced fresh dill

¼ teaspoon kosher salt

4 cups arugula

1. In a medium bowl, combine the chickpeas, shallot, lemon zest and juice, oil, chives, basil, dill, and salt, tossing to mix.

2. To serve, divide the arugula into four (1-cup) portions and spoon the chickpea mixture on top.

 VARIATION: If arugula isn't your favorite green, try this salad wrapped up in crisp iceberg lettuce leaves.

Per serving: Calories: 164; Protein: 5g; Total carbs: 17g; Sugars: 4g; Fiber: 5g; Total fat: 9g; Saturated fat: 1g; Cholesterol: 0mg; Sodium: 217mg

White Bean Panzanella Salad

Serves 4 • Prep time: 10 minutes • Cook time: 10 minutes

DAIRY-FREE • FEW INGREDIENTS • ONE PAN • UNDER 30 MINUTES • VEGETARIAN

There are two foods I could eat every day: bread and tomatoes. Panzanella has both. It's a salad created to use up stale bread. I work hard to keep food waste to a minimum, and this is a great salad to use up any leftover bread or fresh veggies you might have sitting around.

2 cups cubed whole-wheat hearty bread or baguette

2 tablespoons extra-virgin olive oil, divided

2 large vine-ripened tomatoes, cut into bite-size pieces

1 small red onion, very thinly sliced

1 (15-ounce) can cannellini beans, drained and rinsed

¼ cup chopped fresh basil

¼ teaspoon kosher salt

⅛ teaspoon black pepper

1. Preheat the oven to 400°F. Line a baking sheet with aluminum foil.

2. Spread the bread cubes out on the prepared baking sheet and toss with 1 tablespoon of oil. Bake for 10 minutes, or until the bread is golden brown.

3. Place the tomatoes, onions, and beans in a medium serving bowl. Add the warm bread, basil, salt, black pepper, and remaining 1 tablespoon of oil, tossing to combine. Serve immediately.

 COOKING TIP: Once you've combined all the ingredients, this salad is best eaten right away. If you want to take it on the go, pack the bread and vegetables separately and assemble right before eating.

Per serving: Calories: 219; Protein: 8g; Total carbs: 29g; Sugars: 5g; Fiber: 6g; Total fat: 8g; Saturated fat: 1g; Cholesterol: 0mg; Sodium: 293mg

Fattoush

Serves 4 ♦ Prep time: 10 minutes ♦ Cook time: 5 minutes

DAIRY-FREE ♦ UNDER 30 MINUTES ♦ VEGETARIAN

Fattoush is to the Middle East as panzanella is to southern Europe—except that it's made with pita instead of bread cubes. Traditionally, it is drenched in a dressing made with sumac, a red spice that adds a tangy flavor. Sumac is not easy to find, so I add a tangy lemon vinaigrette instead. Dress the salad 10 minutes before you serve it. This will allow the lettuce to wilt slightly and the pita to start absorbing the dressing. It's a salad you'll want to make over and over again.

FOR THE SALAD

2 whole-wheat pitas, cut into bite-size triangles

2 tablespoons extra-virgin olive oil

1 small head iceberg lettuce, chopped (about 8 cups)

1 large tomato, chopped

1 Persian or English cucumber, chopped

FOR THE DRESSING

2 tablespoons freshly squeezed lemon juice

2 tablespoons extra-virgin olive oil

1 teaspoon honey

1 garlic clove, minced

5 mint leaves, minced

½ teaspoon kosher salt

¼ teaspoon black pepper

TO MAKE THE SALAD

1. Preheat the oven to 450°F. Line a baking sheet with aluminum foil.

2. Place the pita triangles on the prepared baking sheet and toss with the oil. Bake for 3 to 5 minutes, until brown and crispy. Place the lettuce, tomato, and cucumber in a large serving bowl. Add the pita crisps.

TO MAKE THE DRESSING

3. Combine the lemon juice, oil, honey, garlic, mint, salt, and black pepper in a small covered container and shake to mix.

4. Toss the salad with the dressing 10 minutes before serving.

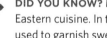 **DID YOU KNOW?** Mint is a popular herb in Middle Eastern cuisine. In the United States, mint is typically used to garnish sweet dishes and desserts, but in other parts of the world, it is used in savory dishes such as this one.

Per serving: Calories: 222; Protein: 4g; Total carbs: 23g; Sugars: 5g; Fiber: 4g; Total fat: 14g; Saturated fat: 2g; Cholesterol: 0mg; Sodium: 429mg

Antipasto Salad

Serves 4 • Prep time: 15 minutes

GLUTEN-FREE • UNDER 30 MINUTES • VEGETARIAN

The true name for this salad should be "end of the week salad," because you take all the ingredients you have left in your refrigerator and add them to a bowl. Salads like this help you use up leftover ingredients from other Mediterranean recipes, like olives, sun-dried tomatoes, and cheese. Mix it up with a super flavorful dressing, and you've got yourself one delicious salad.

FOR THE SALAD

1 head romaine
  lettuce, chopped

12 olives

8 pepperoncini peppers

¼ cup julienned sun-dried
  tomatoes in oil, drained

1 cup halved cherry tomatoes

4 ounces mozzarella cheese,
  cut into ½-inch cubes

FOR THE DRESSING

3 tablespoons extra-virgin
  olive oil

2 tablespoons red
  wine vinegar

1 teaspoon Dijon mustard

½ teaspoon kosher salt

½ teaspoon Italian seasoning

TO MAKE THE SALAD

1. Combine the lettuce, olives, peppers, sun-dried tomatoes, cherry tomatoes, and cheese in a large serving bowl.

TO MAKE THE DRESSING

2. Combine the oil, vinegar, mustard, salt, and Italian seasoning in a small container with a lid and shake to combine.

3. Pour the dressing over the salad and serve.

 VARIATION: This salad is what you make it. If you have extra vegetables in the refrigerator, chop them up and add those to your salad.

Per serving: Calories: 253; Protein: 9g; Total carbs: 13g; Sugars: 4g; Fiber: 5g; Total fat: 20g; Saturated fat: 6g; Cholesterol: 25mg; Sodium: 946mg

Five-Ingredient Naked French Onion Soup

Serves 4 ◆ Prep time: 5 minutes ◆ Cook time: 30 minutes

DAIRY-FREE ◆ FEW INGREDIENTS ◆ GLUTEN-FREE ◆ ONE POT

Most French onion soups are finished with a slice of French bread smothered in Swiss cheese, but I've left that out so the flavors of the soup can really sing and the recipe is extra heart-healthy. Plus, I think this recipe pairs much better with a beautiful and crisp salad.

3 tablespoons extra-virgin olive oil

8 onions, thinly sliced

¼ teaspoon kosher salt

4 cups low-sodium beef stock

1½ tablespoons Worcestershire sauce

1 teaspoon Italian seasoning

1. In a medium Dutch oven or deep skillet over low heat, combine the oil, onions, and salt and cover. Cook the onions for 25 minutes, lifting the cover to stir every 3 minutes, until they have cooked down and start to lightly brown.

2. Add the stock, Worcestershire sauce, and Italian seasoning and bring to a simmer, then serve.

 COOKING TIP: This soup requires a bit of patience. It can be tempting to turn up that heat on the onions, but low and slow is what will caramelize them without burning them.

Per serving: Calories: 203; Protein: 4g; Total carbs: 24g; Sugars: 11g; Fiber: 3g; Total fat: 11g; Saturated fat: 2g; Cholesterol: 5mg; Sodium: 288mg

Potato and Leek Soup

Serves 4 • Prep time: 10 minutes • Cook time: 20 minutes

GLUTEN-FREE • ONE POT • VEGETARIAN

It is a misconception that you can't eat potatoes while following a weight loss plan. They are full of goodness—although certain cooking methods rob them of their nutrients. This soup retains those nutrients and adds plenty of Mediterranean flavor with leek, onion, and garlic. The result is a creamy and comforting soup.

2 tablespoons extra-virgin olive oil

1 leek, white and light green parts only, thinly sliced and thoroughly cleaned (see Cooking tip, below)

1 small onion, chopped

2 garlic cloves, minced

4 Yukon Gold potatoes, cut into ½-inch cubes (about 4 cups)

4 cups low-sodium vegetable broth

½ teaspoon kosher salt

⅛ teaspoon black pepper

4 tablespoons plain full-fat Greek yogurt

1. In a medium Dutch oven or deep skillet over medium heat, combine the oil, leek, onion, and garlic. Sauté for 3 to 4 minutes, until the onions are soft.

2. Add the potatoes, broth, salt, and black pepper. Turn heat to high and boil for 10 to 15 minutes, or until the potatoes are soft.

3. Remove from the heat and puree half the soup, either with an immersion blender or by transferring half the soup to a standing blender. Add the blended soup back to the Dutch oven and stir to combine.

4. Top each serving with 1 tablespoon of Greek yogurt and serve.

❖ **COOKING TIP:** Leeks are grown in sandy soil, which means they have dirt between their layers. To clean a leek, cut the dark green parts off and discard or add them to your compost bin. Slice the white and light green parts and put them in a bowl filled with water. The dirt will fall to the bottom when they soak and break apart. When they are clean, just scoop the leeks off the top and discard the dirty water.

Per serving: Calories: 227; Protein: 6g; Total carbs: 35g; Sugars: 6g; Fiber: 3g; Total fat: 8g; Saturated fat: 1g; Cholesterol: 2mg; Sodium: 296mg

Fast Minestrone

Serves 4 ♦ Prep time: 5 minutes ♦ Cook time: 15 minutes

GLUTEN-FREE ♦ ONE POT ♦ UNDER 30 MINUTES ♦ VEGETARIAN

This one-pot classic Italian soup is one of the quickest meals you can pull together on a weeknight. It uses a mix of fresh and canned ingredients that you probably have on hand all the time. Leaving out the pasta makes it a perfect option for leftovers, as soup only gets better on the second day. However, if you need to feed a crowd, this recipe can easily be doubled, or you can add extra beans or pasta to give the soup more bulk.

2 tablespoons extra-virgin olive oil

1 small onion, finely chopped

1 large carrot, finely chopped

1 celery stalk, finely chopped

1 garlic clove, minced

½ teaspoon Italian seasoning

½ teaspoon kosher salt

¼ teaspoon black pepper

1 (14-ounce) can diced tomatoes

1 (15-ounce) can cannellini beans, drained and rinsed

4 cups low-sodium vegetable broth

3 cups chopped baby spinach

¼ cup freshly grated Parmesan cheese

1. In a medium Dutch oven, deep skillet, or pot over medium-high heat, combine the oil, onion, carrot, and celery and sauté, stirring occasionally, for 3 to 4 minutes, until the onions are translucent. Add the garlic, Italian seasoning, salt, and black pepper and stir.

2. Add the tomatoes, beans, and broth and turn the heat to medium-low. Let the soup simmer for 10 minutes. Stir in the spinach and allow to wilt, about 2 minutes.

3. Garnish each serving with 1 tablespoon of Parmesan cheese and serve.

 SUBSTITUTION TIP: If you have frozen vegetables, such as spinach or carrots, you can use them in place of fresh.

Per serving: Calories: 237; Protein: 11g; Total carbs: 27g; Sugars: 7g; Fiber: 8g; Total fat: 10g; Saturated fat: 2g; Cholesterol: 5mg; Sodium: 649mg

Carrot, Chickpea, and Quinoa Soup

Serves 4 ◆ Prep time: 5 minutes ◆ Cook time: 25 minutes

DAIRY-FREE ◆ GLUTEN-FREE ◆ VEGAN

Mediterranean cooking is so diverse. It can be nice to take a break from the traditional flavors of southern Europe and go farther south to the flavors of North Africa. The spices used in this soup are used in many other recipes in this book, including Moroccan-Inspired Beef with Couscous (page 156).

2 tablespoons extra-virgin olive oil

1 large carrot, finely chopped

1 onion, finely chopped

1 (15-ounce) can chickpeas, drained and rinsed

2 garlic cloves, minced

1 teaspoon ground cumin

1 teaspoon ground coriander

½ teaspoon kosher salt

¼ teaspoon ground cinnamon

¼ teaspoon red pepper flakes

½ cup quinoa

3½ cups low-sodium vegetable broth, divided

1. In a medium Dutch oven or deep skillet over medium heat, combine the oil, carrot, onion, and chickpeas and sauté for 3 to 4 minutes, until the onions are translucent. Stir in the garlic, cumin, coriander, salt, cinnamon, and red pepper flakes.

2. Remove 2 cups of this vegetable mixture from the pot and set aside.

3. Add the quinoa and 3 cups of broth to the pot, cover, and bring to a boil.

4. Place the 2 cups of reserved vegetables and the remaining ½ cup of broth in a blender and blend until smooth. Add it back into the soup pot, cover, and turn the heat to low.

5. Simmer for 10 to 15 minutes, or until the quinoa has puffed up. Serve.

 DID YOU KNOW? Quinoa is a complete protein. That means it contains all nine essential amino acids, which is rare in a plant protein. You also get fiber—you won't find that in meat.

Per serving: Calories: 263; Protein: 9g; Total carbs: 36g; Sugars: 7g; Fiber: 7g; Total fat: 10g; Saturated fat: 1g; Cholesterol: 0mg; Sodium: 415mg

Turkey Sausage and Pasta Soup

Serves 4 • Prep time: 5 minutes • Cook time: 25 minutes

ONE POT

My family loves this soup, and it comes together so quickly. Mini penne or bowtie pasta works well here for the pasta. If you do not care for spicy food, go for the regular turkey sausage. While the soup is simmering, I like to fix up a Weeknight Garden Salad with Vinaigrette (page 90) to serve as an accompaniment.

8 ounces spicy Italian turkey sausage, casings removed

2 tablespoons extra-virgin olive oil

1 large carrot, chopped

1 onion, chopped

3 garlic cloves, smashed

2 (15-ounce) cans fire-roasted tomatoes, divided

1½ cups water

1 cup pasta of choice

¼ teaspoon kosher salt

½ teaspoon Italian seasoning

¼ cup freshly grated Parmesan cheese

1. In a medium Dutch oven or deep skillet over medium heat, break up the turkey sausage with a wooden spoon. Cook for 6 to 7 minutes, until the sausage is brown. Transfer it to a colander and rinse any grease off. Set aside.

2. In the same pot over medium heat, add the oil, carrot, onion, and garlic. Sauté, stirring frequently, for 4 minutes, until they just start to get soft.

3. Transfer the sautéed veggies to a blender and add 1 can of tomatoes. Blend until smooth.

4. Add the puree and cooked sausage back to the pot and add in the remaining can of tomatoes, water, pasta, salt, and Italian seasoning. Cover and simmer for 15 minutes, or until the pasta is cooked.

5. Garnish with the Parmesan cheese and serve.

 COOKING TIP: If your turkey sausage starts to stick to the pan, drizzle 1 additional tablespoon of olive oil into the pan.

Per serving: Calories: 344; Protein: 17g; Total carbs: 36g; Sugars: 8g; Fiber: 5g; Total fat: 15g; Saturated fat: 3g; Cholesterol: 50mg; Sodium: 1204mg

Beef and Lentil Soup

Serves 4 • Prep time: 15 minutes • Cook time: 2½ hours, plus 30 minutes to rest

DAIRY-FREE • GLUTEN-FREE • ONE POT

Comfort never tasted so good. This soup takes a little patience for the beef to become tender, but it's well worth it. The ingredients for this dish are inexpensive and easy to find. Adding lentils boosts the protein to make it a hearty and satisfying meal that doesn't need anything else.

3 tablespoons extra-virgin olive oil

1 onion, sliced

1 pound beef chuck roast, fat trimmed, cut into 1-inch pieces

¾ teaspoon kosher salt

¼ teaspoon black pepper

½ teaspoon paprika

½ teaspoon ground cumin

½ teaspoon ground turmeric

2½ cups low-sodium beef stock

2 garlic cloves, smashed

2 large carrots, cut into 1-inch pieces

2 Yukon Gold or red potatoes, cut into 1-inch pieces

½ cup dried brown lentils

1 cup water

1 tablespoon red wine vinegar

1. Preheat the oven to 325°F.

2. In a Dutch oven, deep skillet, or large ovenproof pot over medium heat combine the oil, onions, and beef. Cook, turning the beef pieces, for about 5 minutes, until they are browned on all sides. Sprinkle the salt, black pepper, paprika, cumin, and turmeric over the beef, then add the stock and garlic.

3. Remove the pot from the heat, cover, and place in the oven for 1½ hours.

4. Uncover, add the carrots, potatoes, lentils, and water, and put the pot back in the oven for 1 hour.

5. Remove the pot from the oven and stir in the vinegar. Let the pot sit, covered, for 30 minutes before serving.

 SUBSTITUTION TIP: You can substitute any color lentil. The lentils help thicken the soup, so don't leave them out.

Per serving: Calories: 545; Protein: 31g; Total carbs: 35g; Sugars: 5g; Fiber: 10g; Total fat: 31g; Saturated fat: 9g; Cholesterol: 108mg; Sodium: 626mg

CHAPTER 8

Beans, Eggs, Grains, and Vegetable Mains

Roasted Chickpea and Feta Salad

Serves 4 • Prep time: 10 minutes • Cook time: 10 minutes

GLUTEN-FREE • UNDER 30 MINUTES • VEGETARIAN

This main dish salad is one I make so frequently that I don't even have to add the ingredients to my shopping list; they just automatically make it into the shopping cart. This salad is the epitome of plant-based eating and is sure to fill you up. It is loaded with vegetables and an olive oil dressing with fresh dill. I always roast my chickpeas for this salad, but if you're short on time, skip that step.

1 (15-ounce) can chickpeas, drained and rinsed

3 tablespoons extra-virgin olive oil, divided

2 large tomatoes, cut into ½-inch cubes

1 cucumber, cut into ½-inch cubes

1 small zucchini, chopped

1 cup quartered radishes

½ cup sliced red onions

½ cup Kalamata olives

1 tablespoon freshly squeezed lemon juice

2 tablespoons minced fresh dill

½ teaspoon kosher salt

⅛ teaspoon black pepper

4 ounces crumbled feta cheese

1. Preheat the oven to 400°F. Line a baking sheet with parchment paper.

2. Spread the chickpeas on the prepared baking sheet and toss with 1 tablespoon of oil. Roast for 10 minutes, or until the chickpeas are golden brown but still soft.

3. Transfer them to a large serving bowl. Add the tomatoes, cucumber, zucchini, radishes, onions, and olives.

4. In a small bowl, whisk together the remaining 2 tablespoons of oil, lemon juice, dill, salt, and black pepper. Pour over the salad.

5. Scatter the feta on top, then serve immediately.

 COOKING TIP: If you're making this ahead or taking it to a potluck, leave the dressing off until you are ready to eat it. Otherwise, the salt in the dressing will pull the water out of the vegetables and leave too much liquid in the bottom of your bowl.

Per serving: Calories: 331; Protein: 11g; Total carbs: 27g; Sugars: 10g; Fiber: 8g; Total fat: 22g; Saturated fat: 6g; Cholesterol: 25mg; Sodium: 937mg

Roasted Cauliflower and Broccoli Hummus Bowl with Pita

Serves 4 ♦ Prep time: 10 minutes ♦ Cook time: 25 minutes

ONE PAN ♦ VEGETARIAN

There is a lot of debate about the origins of hummus. Some will say it originated in the Middle East, others say Egypt. Either way, it's a favorite in the Mediterranean. The popularity of protein-packed chickpeas makes them a staple. Hummus bowls are a modern spin on simply dipping your raw veggies into a container of hummus.

1 small head cauliflower, cut into bite-size florets

1 small broccoli crown, cut into bite-size florets

1 red onion, sliced

2 tablespoons extra-virgin olive oil

½ teaspoon kosher salt

¼ teaspoon black pepper

1⅓ cups prepared hummus or Roasted Garlic Hummus (page 84)

1 small cucumber, thinly sliced

½ cup plain full-fat Greek yogurt

4 whole-wheat pita rounds, cut into wedges

Pinch red pepper flakes (optional)

1. Preheat the oven to 425°F. Line a baking sheet with aluminum foil.

2. Put the cauliflower, broccoli, and onion on the prepared baking sheet and toss with the oil, salt, and black pepper.

3. Roast for 20 to 25 minutes, or until the vegetables start to brown and get soft.

4. In each bowl, add ⅓ cup of hummus, some roasted veggies, cucumber, 2 tablespoons of yogurt, and one pita.

5. Add red pepper flakes (if using) to each bowl right before serving.

 VARIATION: Having your food in a bowl gives you the freedom to add and subtract any ingredients you have at home. A sprinkle of nuts or switching the cucumbers for tomatoes are ways for you to keep your meals interesting and never have the same thing twice.

Per serving: Calories: 466; Protein: 17g; Total carbs: 57g; Sugars: 7g; Fiber: 10g; Total fat: 21g; Saturated fat: 3g; Cholesterol: 5mg; Sodium: 1060mg

Mushroom and Pea Orzotto

Serves 4 ◆ Prep time: 5 minutes ◆ Cook time: 20 minutes

ONE POT ◆ UNDER 30 MINUTES ◆ VEGETARIAN

The most popular rice dish in Italy is risotto, but it takes time and a dedicated stirring hand to get the creamy texture that is characteristic of good risotto. If you have the time to devote to risotto, it's worth it. But if time is not on your side, this "orzotto" is a perfect substitute. Using orzo pasta instead of rice gives you a dish that resembles the creamy texture of risotto. Grate the Parmesan fresh for this dish, if you can.

2 tablespoons extra-virgin olive oil

1 small red onion, chopped

1 pound white button mushrooms, sliced

2 garlic cloves, minced

1 cup orzo pasta

2 cups low-sodium vegetable broth (or 2 cups water mixed with ½ teaspoon kosher salt)

2 cups frozen peas

½ cup freshly grated Parmesan cheese

1. In a large skillet over medium heat, combine the oil, onion, and mushrooms and sauté for 10 minutes, or until the mushrooms start to brown. Add the garlic and orzo and sauté for 1 minute.

2. Add the broth, turn the heat to low, and simmer, stirring occasionally, for 10 minutes.

3. Stir in the peas and Parmesan. Serve warm.

 SUBSTITUTION TIP: If you can't find a block of Parmesan in the grocery store to grate or want to save some money, look for Grana Padano. It tastes very similar to Parmesan, is made in Italy, and is cheaper.

Per serving: Calories: 374; Protein: 17g; Total carbs: 52g; Sugars: 9g; Fiber: 10g; Total fat: 11g; Saturated fat: 3g; Cholesterol: 11mg; Sodium: 392mg

Roasted Butternut Squash with Almond, Apricot, and Rosemary Couscous

Serves 4 • Prep time: 5 minutes • Cook time: 30 minutes
VEGETARIAN

Mediterranean recipes are naturally easy with fresh ingredients, and this one certainly fits that criteria. Butternut squash is typically a winter fruit, but you can find it fresh all year round in most grocery stores—or in the freezer section. Yes, you can use a bag of peeled and diced butternut squash for this recipe, and no one has to know.

1 small butternut squash, seeded and cut into bite-size pieces

4 tablespoons extra-virgin olive oil, divided

⅓ cup sliced unsalted almonds

12 dried apricots, chopped

1½ cups couscous

1½ cups water

1 tablespoon finely chopped fresh rosemary

½ cup freshly grated Parmesan cheese

⅛ teaspoon kosher salt

1. Preheat the oven to 425°F. Line a baking sheet with parchment paper.

2. Arrange the butternut squash in a single layer on the prepared baking sheet and toss with 2 tablespoons of oil. Roast for 20 minutes, or until the butternut squash is soft.

3. While the squash is cooking, place the almonds in a small Dutch oven or deep skillet over medium heat and toast for 1 to 2 minutes, until brown.

4. Add the apricots, couscous, water, rosemary, and the remaining 2 tablespoons of oil and cover the pot. Simmer for 5 minutes, then remove from the heat. Let sit for 5 minutes, then fluff the couscous with a fork.

5. When the squash is done roasting, add it to the couscous and gently mix together. Sprinkle with the Parmesan and salt and serve.

 DID YOU KNOW? You can keep the skin on your butternut squash when you roast it. This makes it so much easier and saves time when prepping—plus eating it gives you an extra serving of fiber.

Per serving: Calories: 555; Protein: 16g; Total carbs: 77g; Sugars: 10g; Fiber: 10g; Total fat: 22g; Saturated fat: 4g; Cholesterol: 11mg; Sodium: 275mg

Smoky Rice and Beans with Avocado and Lime

Serves 4 ◆ Prep time: 5 minutes ◆ Cook time: 30 minutes

DAIRY-FREE ◆ GLUTEN-FREE ◆ ONE PAN ◆ VEGAN

Rice and beans is one of my favorite dishes. While the combination of rice and black beans is not a combination you will see near the Mediterranean, pairings of grains with legumes are extremely common. The combination of rice with beans makes a complete protein, which provides all nine essential amino acids to the body without meat.

2 tablespoons extra-virgin olive oil

1 onion, finely chopped

2 garlic cloves, minced

1 teaspoon smoked paprika

1 teaspoon ground turmeric

1 teaspoon kosher salt

½ teaspoon black pepper

1 cup short-grain rice, such as bomba or arborio

3 cups water

1 (15-ounce) can black beans, drained and rinsed

1 avocado, sliced

1 scallion, white and green parts, thinly sliced

1 lime, cut into wedges

1. In a large skillet over medium heat, combine the oil, onion, garlic, paprika, turmeric, salt, and black pepper. Sauté for 1 to 2 minutes, or until the garlic is fragrant, being careful not to burn it.

2. Turn the heat to low, add the rice, water, and beans, and simmer for 25 minutes.

3. Divide the rice into four serving bowls and add the avocado and scallion on top. Squeeze a lime wedge over each bowl of rice and serve.

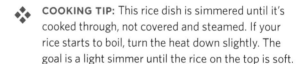 **COOKING TIP:** This rice dish is simmered until it's cooked through, not covered and steamed. If your rice starts to boil, turn the heat down slightly. The goal is a light simmer until the rice on the top is soft.

Per serving: Calories: 415; Protein: 12g; Total carbs: 66g; Sugars: 2g; Fiber: 14g; Total fat: 13g; Saturated fat: 2g; Cholesterol: 0mg; Sodium: 595mg

Farro with Cucumbers, White Beans, and Lemon

Serves 4 ✦ Prep time: 5 minutes ✦ Cook time: 30 minutes

DAIRY-FREE ✦ VEGAN

Farro might be the new darling of the grain world, which means it's easier than ever to find in your grocery store. If it's not in the pasta and rice aisle near the rest of the grains, check out the natural foods section. The chewy texture and nuttiness of farro is unexpectedly delightful and a surprising hit with kids. If you're making this ahead of time, hold off on adding the vinaigrette until you're ready to eat. That will keep everything crisp and fresh.

FOR THE DRESSING

Zest and juice of 1 lemon

2 tablespoons extra-virgin olive oil

2 tablespoons white wine vinegar

1 teaspoon Dijon mustard

1 teaspoon kosher salt

2 tablespoons chopped fresh dill, or 2 teaspoons dried dill

FOR THE FARRO

3 cups water (or as package recommends)

1 cup farro

1 small cucumber, cut into ½-inch cubes

1 (15-ounce) can cannellini beans, drained and rinsed

2 cups arugula

TO MAKE THE DRESSING

1. Put the lemon zest and juice, oil, vinegar, mustard, salt, and dill in a small covered container and shake to mix.

TO MAKE THE FARRO

2. Cook the farro according to the package directions. The standard method is to put the water and farro in a medium saucepan, bring it to a boil, turn the heat to low, and simmer for 30 minutes. Drain.

3. Add the cucumber and beans to a serving bowl. Add the drained farro.

4. Add the dressing and toss, then add the arugula and toss again. Serve immediately.

 SUBSTITUTION TIP: If you are gluten-free or you don't have farro on hand, substitute the same amount of uncooked quinoa for the farro. Just follow the cooking instructions on the package.

Per serving: Calories: 331; Protein: 13g; Total carbs: 55g; Sugars: 3g; Fiber: 12g; Total fat: 9g; Saturated fat: 1g; Cholesterol: 0mg; Sodium: 660mg

Roasted Vegetable and Chickpea Bowl with Farro

Serves 4 • Prep time: 10 minutes • Cook time: 30 minutes
VEGETARIAN

Roasted vegetables are an essential part of Mediterranean cuisine. You might find yourself roasting a pan of eggplant, zucchini, bell peppers, and/or tomatoes and adding them to just about everything. If you're making extras for leftovers, make sure you pack the feta and pine nuts together in a separate small container, to keep them fresh until you are ready to eat.

1 cup farro

3 cups water

1 zucchini, cut into ½-inch cubes

1 eggplant, cut into ½-inch cubes

2 red onions, cut into big pieces

1 (15-ounce) can chickpeas, drained and rinsed

2 tablespoons extra-virgin olive oil

3 tablespoons balsamic vinegar, divided

1 teaspoon kosher salt

4 ounces feta cheese, crumbled

¼ cup pine nuts

1. Preheat the oven to 425°F. Line a baking sheet with parchment paper.

2. Put the farro and water in a medium saucepan over high heat. Bring to a boil, turn the heat to low, and simmer, uncovered, for 30 minutes.

3. While the farro is cooking, spread the zucchini, eggplant, onions, and chickpeas on the prepared baking sheet and toss with the oil, 2 tablespoons of vinegar, and salt. Roast for 15 minutes, remove from the oven, and drizzle with the remaining 1 tablespoon of vinegar.

4. Add ¾ cup of cooked farro to each of four bowls and pile them with veggies. Top each bowl with 1 ounce of feta cheese and 1 tablespoon of pine nuts.

 DID YOU KNOW? One ounce of feta cheese is going to give you about the same amount of calcium (140mg) as you'll get in 1 cup of cottage cheese. That's pretty good!

Per serving: Calories: 527; Protein: 19g; Total carbs: 72g; Sugars: 15g; Fiber: 17g; Total fat: 21g; Saturated fat: 6g; Cholesterol: 25mg; Sodium: 763mg

Primavera Vegetable and Quinoa Bowl

Serves 4 • Prep time: 10 minutes • Cook time: 25 minutes

GLUTEN-FREE • VEGETARIAN

Pasta with vegetables is a dish you will find in many Mediterranean cuisines—each one with a slightly different twist. This version of a primavera swaps out the pasta for quinoa, for a very of-the-moment grain bowl. Quinoa has more protein, iron, and fiber than you will get from pasta.

1 cup quinoa

1¾ cups water

3 tablespoons extra-virgin olive oil, divided

8 ounces broccoli, florets and stems, chopped into bite-size pieces (about 3 cups)

1 red bell pepper, cut into bite-size pieces

1 large carrot, thinly sliced

½ teaspoon kosher salt

¾ teaspoon Italian seasoning, divided

¼ teaspoon red pepper flakes

4 cups halved cherry tomatoes

1 (10-ounce) bag baby spinach

¼ cup shelled unsalted pistachios

¼ cup freshly grated Parmesan cheese

1. To make the quinoa, in a medium saucepan over high heat, combine the quinoa and water. Bring to a boil, then turn the heat to low, cover, and simmer for 15 minutes, or until the quinoa has absorbed all the water. Remove from the heat and fluff with a fork.

2. In a large skillet over medium heat, warm 2 tablespoons of oil. Add the broccoli, bell pepper, and carrot and sauté, stirring occasionally, for 10 minutes, until the veggies just start to soften (you still want some crunch). Add the salt, ½ teaspoon of Italian seasoning, and the red pepper flakes.

3. Place the tomatoes in a small bowl with the remaining 1 tablespoon of oil and remaining ¼ teaspoon of Italian seasoning and mix gently.

4. To assemble the bowls, add ½ cup of cooked quinoa, 1 cup of vegetables, 1 cup of seasoned tomatoes, and 1 cup of baby spinach to each bowl. Top each one with 1 tablespoon of pistachios and 1 tablespoon of Parmesan cheese. Serve.

 VARIATION: If you have any vinaigrette left over from another salad, drizzle a little over the top of this for an extra flavor boost.

Per serving: Calories: 410; Protein: 15g; Total carbs: 50g; Sugars: 9g; Fiber: 11g; Total fat: 18g; Saturated fat: 3g; Cholesterol: 5mg; Sodium: 506mg

Peppers Skillet with Lentils and Feta

Serves 4 ◆ Prep time: 5 minutes ◆ Cook time: 30 minutes

GLUTEN-FREE ◆ ONE PAN ◆ VEGETARIAN

Stuffed peppers is a classic dish that is served in every type of Mediterranean cuisine. One major downside to stuffed peppers is the long cooking time involved. This skillet is a one-pan variation that uses many of the elements of stuffed peppers but is a lot faster—with a vegetarian twist of lentils instead of beef.

2 tablespoons extra-virgin olive oil

1 large tomato, chopped

1 small onion, chopped

1 small green bell pepper, chopped

1 small yellow bell pepper, chopped

2 garlic cloves, minced

½ teaspoon kosher salt

½ teaspoon Italian seasoning

¼ teaspoon red pepper flakes

½ cup short-grain rice, such as bomba or arborio

¼ cup dried brown lentils

2½ cups low-sodium vegetable broth

2 ounces crumbled feta cheese

1. In a medium skillet over medium heat, add the oil, tomato, onion, green and yellow bell peppers, and garlic. Sauté for 10 minutes, stirring every 2 minutes, until the veggies just soften.

2. Add the salt, Italian seasoning, red pepper flakes, rice, lentils, and broth. Turn the heat to low and simmer, uncovered, for 20 minutes. Remove from the heat and fluff the rice with a fork.

3. To serve, crumble the feta over the top.

 COOKING TIP: To keep the rice from releasing its starch and becoming creamy, do not stir it once you add it to the skillet. If the water is evaporating too quickly, simply turn down the heat. Always fluff your rice with a fork when it's done cooking, rather than stirring.

Per serving: Calories: 255; Protein: 9g; Total carbs: 33g; Sugars: 4g; Fiber: 6g; Total fat: 10g; Saturated fat: 3g; Cholesterol: 13mg; Sodium: 392mg

Pizza with Pesto, Mushrooms, and Spinach

Serves 4 • Prep time: 15 minutes, plus 1 hour to rise • Cook time: 20 minutes

VEGETARIAN

Pizza is a quintessential Mediterranean food, so you can't have a cookbook like this without a recipe for it. Many are surprised that it can be made minus all the saturated fat and excess calories. This recipe uses whole-wheat flour, but can be made with only all-purpose flour if that's all you have. You will find that the gluten in all-purpose flour yields a chewier crust and the whole-wheat flour is denser, but full of fiber—and flavor.

1 teaspoon active dry yeast

¾ cup warm water

1 cup whole-wheat flour

½ cup all-purpose flour

½ teaspoon kosher salt

Nonstick cooking spray

½ cup basil pesto

½ cup freshly grated
  Parmesan cheese

10 white button mushrooms,
  thinly sliced

1 cup packed baby spinach

1. In a large bowl, combine the yeast and warm water and let it sit for 2 minutes. Add the whole-wheat and all-purpose flours and salt and mix together to form a ball. Cover and let rest for 1 hour.

2. Preheat the oven to 450°F. Spray a pizza pan or baking sheet with nonstick cooking spray.

3. Put the dough in the pan and use your hands to spread it out until it is about ⅛-inch thick. Pinch the dough all around the perimeter to form a crust.

4. Spread the pesto over the dough, then layer on the Parmesan cheese, mushrooms, and spinach.

5. Bake for 15 to 20 minutes, or until the outer edges of the crust are golden brown. Serve.

 COOKING TIP: If you have trouble spreading out the dough, put a little olive oil on your fingertips before you start shaping it on the pan, and that should stop any sticking.

Per serving: Calories: 338; Protein: 12g; Total carbs: 39g; Sugars: 2g; Fiber: 5g; Total fat: 16g; Saturated fat: 4g; Cholesterol: 11mg; Sodium: 693mg

Easy Falafel with Spicy Avocado Sauce

Serves 4 • Prep time: 10 minutes • Cook time: 20 minutes

DAIRY-FREE • VEGAN

Traditional falafel is made with dried chickpeas that must be soaked. Soaking takes time—about eight hours to be exact—and even though it's all passive time, when you want falafel, an eight-hour soak isn't going to happen. I get around the extra moisture in canned chickpeas by using a little flour. I also bumped up the health factor by baking these falafels instead of deep-frying. Getting a good brush of olive oil on both sides yields a crispy exterior, and you'll never miss the fryer.

FOR THE FALAFEL

1 (15-ounce) can chickpeas, drained and rinsed

¼ cup chopped fresh parsley

¼ cup chopped fresh cilantro

1 small shallot

1 garlic clove

½ teaspoon kosher salt

½ teaspoon ground cumin

¼ cup all-purpose flour

1 tablespoon extra-virgin olive oil

FOR THE SAUCE

1 teaspoon extra-virgin olive oil

1 small jalapeño pepper, chopped

1 small shallot, chopped

1 avocado, halved, pitted, and peeled

2 tablespoons chopped fresh cilantro

¼ teaspoon kosher salt

TO MAKE THE FALAFEL

1. Preheat the oven to 400°F. Line a baking sheet with parchment paper.

2. Put the chickpeas, parsley, cilantro, shallot, garlic, salt, and cumin in a blender and pulse until the mixture is chopped and comes together. This may take a little scraping down. You'll know it's done when you can press the mixture with the back of a spoon and it comes together. Scrape the mixture into a large bowl and mix with the flour.

3. Scoop up about 2 tablespoons of the falafel mixture and roll it into a ball, then press and hand-form it into a disc. Set on the parchment paper. Repeat with the entire mixture. You should have 12 falafels.

4. Brush the oil all over the falafels. Bake for 10 minutes, until they're lightly browned on the bottom. Flip and bake for another 10 minutes, until the falafels are golden brown.

TO MAKE THE SAUCE

5. While the falafel bakes, make the sauce. Place the oil, jalapeño, shallot, avocado, cilantro, and salt in a clean blender and pulse until smooth.

6. Serve the falafel with the sauce for dipping.

❖ **SUBSTITUTION TIP:** Avocado sauce is not traditional for falafel. If you'd like something a little cooler, try the tzatziki (page 85) as a sauce for this recipe.

Per serving (3 falafels and ¼ cup sauce): Calories: 237; Protein: 7g; Total carbs: 28g; Sugars: 5g; Fiber: 8g; Total fat: 12g; Saturated fat: 2g; Cholesterol: 0mg; Sodium: 360mg

Orecchiette with Spinach Pesto and Butternut Squash

Serves 4 ✦ Prep time: 5 minutes ✦ Cook time: 20 minutes

UNDER 30 MINUTES ✦ VEGETARIAN

Pasta is an Italian staple, but portion control can be a challenge. Accordingly, this recipe showcases the veggies more than the pasta. You can keep the skin on the butternut squash or you can take it off. If you're going to leave it on, make sure you wash your squash before you start cutting. Serve this with a green salad and a bowl of fresh seasonal fruit.

FOR THE PESTO

2 cups packed baby spinach

¼ cup walnuts

1 tablespoon freshly squeezed lemon juice

½ teaspoon kosher salt

2 tablespoons extra-virgin olive oil

FOR THE PASTA

1 small butternut squash, seeded and cut into bite-size pieces

2 tablespoons extra-virgin olive oil

¼ teaspoon kosher salt

¼ teaspoon black pepper

1½ cups whole-wheat orecchiette pasta

⅓ cup chopped walnuts

½ cup freshly grated Parmesan cheese

TO MAKE THE PESTO

1. In a blender, combine the spinach, walnuts, lemon juice, salt, and oil and blend until smooth. Set aside.

TO MAKE THE PASTA

2. Preheat the oven to 425°F. Line a baking sheet with parchment paper.

3. Arrange the butternut squash in a single layer on the prepared baking sheet and toss with the oil, salt, and black pepper. Roast for 20 minutes, or until the butternut squash is soft.

4. While the squash is roasting, cook the pasta according to the package directions.

5. When the pasta is done, drain and transfer it to a serving bowl. Toss with the pesto, butternut squash, and chopped walnuts. Sprinkle each serving with Parmesan cheese, then serve.

❖ **VARIATION:** Orecchiette are shaped like little ears and hold a sauce well, but any type of pasta with ridges will also hold on to a sauce. If you can't find the whole-wheat orecchiette, look for whole-wheat penne or cavatappi.

Per serving: Calories: 468; Protein: 13g; Total carbs: 44g; Sugars: 4g; Fiber: 6g; Total fat: 29g; Saturated fat: 5g; Cholesterol: 11mg; Sodium: 451mg

Roasted Tomato and Onion Soup with Garlic Toast and Salad

Serves 4 • Prep time: 15 minutes • Cook time: 25 minutes

DAIRY-FREE • VEGETARIAN

It can be hard to pull together a main dish and side dishes without feeling like you're spending hours in the kitchen, and if you don't like to meal prep, pulling an entire meal together may feel like a chore instead of fun. This is a complete meal, meant to carry you through at least one weeknight. But this soup couldn't be easier—you cook everything in the oven and blend it up.

FOR THE SOUP

2 pounds ripe tomatoes, cut into big pieces

1 red onion, sliced

3 garlic cloves, peeled

2 tablespoons extra-virgin olive oil

¾ teaspoon kosher salt

¼ teaspoon black pepper

FOR THE TOAST

8 small baguette slices

1 garlic clove, smashed

1 tablespoon extra-virgin olive oil

FOR THE SALAD

1 avocado, cubed

1 (9-ounce) bag field greens

2 scallions, white and green parts, thinly sliced

2 teaspoons extra-virgin olive oil

2 teaspoons freshly squeezed lime juice

¼ teaspoon kosher salt

¼ teaspoon black pepper

TO MAKE THE SOUP

1. Preheat the oven to 400°F. Line two baking sheets with aluminum foil.

2. Place the tomatoes, onion, and garlic on one of the prepared baking sheets and toss with the oil, salt, and black pepper. Roast for 20 minutes, or until the tomatoes are bursting and the onions are soft.

3. Remove the veggies from oven and add them to a blender. Blend until smooth and then transfer them to a saucepan over low heat to keep warm.

TO MAKE THE TOAST

4. While the vegetables roast, place the baguette slices on the other prepared baking sheet. Rub the smashed garlic on the bread, then brush the slices with the oil and set aside.

5. When the veggies are out of the oven, set it to broil and place the bread under the broiler for about 1 minute, until just golden brown.

TO MAKE THE SALAD

6. In a medium serving bowl, place the avocado, greens, scallions, oil, lime juice, salt, and black pepper. Toss to combine.

7. Serve the tomato soup with a side of avocado salad and two pieces of toast per person.

❖❖ **COOKING TIP:** You can make the soup up to three days in advance. It tastes even better when the flavors have some time to meld.

Per serving: Calories: 388; Protein: 9g; Total carbs: 50g; Sugars: 8g; Fiber: 7g; Total fat: 18g; Saturated fat: 3g; Cholesterol: 0mg; Sodium: 696mg

Healthy Tuscan Quiche

Serves 4 ◆ Prep time: 20 minutes, plus 15 minutes to chill ◆ Cook time: 45 minutes

VEGETARIAN

Quiche doesn't have to be off-limits on a weight-loss plan. The main cooking fat in Mediterranean cooking is olive oil, but in some places, they use small amounts of butter, which you need for a piecrust. The crust here is made entirely of whole-wheat flour, with a touch of butter to still give you a classically flaky texture. This recipe gives you a generous slice for dinner but leaves room for a green salad on the side.

FOR THE CRUST

1 cup whole-wheat flour, plus more for dusting

3 tablespoons unsalted butter, cold, cut into small cubes

¼ teaspoon kosher salt

3 tablespoons cold water

FOR THE QUICHE

4 large eggs

1½ cups 2% milk

10 ounces frozen spinach, thawed and liquid squeezed out

½ cup freshly grated Parmesan cheese

¼ teaspoon kosher salt

¼ teaspoon black pepper

¼ teaspoon Italian seasoning

¼ teaspoon red pepper flakes

TO MAKE THE CRUST

1. Place the flour, butter, and salt in a medium bowl and incorporate everything using a fork or a pastry cutter until the butter is the size of peas. Add the water, stir, and then use your hands to work the mixture until the dough just comes together. Form into a disk, wrap it tight in plastic wrap, and chill the dough for 15 minutes.

TO MAKE THE QUICHE

2. While the dough is chilling, in a large bowl, mix together the eggs, milk, spinach, Parmesan cheese, salt, black pepper, Italian seasoning, and red pepper flakes.

3. Preheat the oven to 375°F.

4. Add a small dusting of flour to your countertop so your dough doesn't stick, and roll it out into a 12-inch circle, sprinkling a small amount of flour on the counter and dough if it starts to stick. Gently fit the pie dough into a 9-inch pie plate, and cut off any excess. Pour the quiche mixture into the crust.

5. Bake for 45 minutes, or until the center is set and the top is lightly browned. You'll know the center is set if you give your quiche a little shake before removing it from the oven. If the center jiggles, it needs a few more minutes.

6. Let stand for 10 minutes before serving.

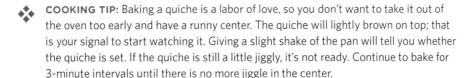 **COOKING TIP:** Baking a quiche is a labor of love, so you don't want to take it out of the oven too early and have a runny center. The quiche will lightly brown on top; that is your signal to start watching it. Giving a slight shake of the pan will tell you whether the quiche is set. If the quiche is still a little jiggly, it's not ready. Continue to bake for 3-minute intervals until there is no more jiggle in the center.

Per serving: Calories: 373; Protein: 21g; Total carbs: 30g; Sugars: 6g; Fiber: 6g; Total fat: 20g; Saturated fat: 10g; Cholesterol: 204mg; Sodium: 697mg

Smoky Shakshuka

Serves 4 ◆ Prep time: 10 minutes ◆ Cook time: 20 minutes

GLUTEN-FREE ◆ ONE PAN ◆ VEGETARIAN

This classic Mediterranean dish can sound intimidating as it differs from standard egg dishes in the United States, but it is surprisingly easy to make. With a little help from the oven, the eggs come out with a perfect softboiled yolk.

2 tablespoons extra-virgin olive oil

1 small red onion, finely chopped

1 small red bell pepper, finely chopped

1 garlic clove, minced

1 (15-ounce) can fire-roasted tomatoes

4 ounces frozen spinach, thawed and liquid squeezed out

¼ teaspoon kosher salt

¼ teaspoon black pepper

¼ teaspoon smoked paprika

4 large eggs

2 ounces crumbled feta cheese

2 tablespoons chopped fresh cilantro

1. Preheat the oven to 350°F.

2. In a large oven-safe skillet over medium heat, combine the oil, onion, and bell pepper and sauté for 5 minutes, until the onions are translucent. Add the garlic and sauté for 1 minute.

3. Transfer the sautéed vegetables to a blender. Add the tomatoes and pulse until everything is blended together.

4. Transfer the tomato mixture back to the skillet and stir in the spinach, salt, black pepper, and paprika.

5. Using a large spoon, make four wells in the tomato sauce and crack an egg in each well.

6. Transfer the skillet to the oven and bake for 10 minutes, or until the whites of the eggs are no longer jiggly. Remove from the oven and top with the feta and cilantro. Serve.

Per serving: Calories: 221; Protein: 11g; Total carbs: 13g; Sugars: 7g; Fiber: 4g; Total fat: 15g; Saturated fat: 4g; Cholesterol: 177mg; Sodium: 570mg

CHAPTER 9

Fish and Seafood Mains

Chickpea and Tuna Salad Lettuce Cups

Serves 4 ◆ Prep time: 10 minutes

GLUTEN-FREE ◆ UNDER 30 MINUTES

This tuna salad is made with Greek yogurt as a healthier alternative to mayonnaise. Serving it in lettuce cups is a fun and low-calorie way to enjoy this salad. If you're packing this to go, separate the tuna salad from the lettuce leaves and assemble them when you're ready to eat.

2 (5-ounce) cans tuna packed in water, drained

1 large shallot, minced

1 celery stalk, finely chopped

1 (15-ounce) can chickpeas, drained and rinsed

¼ cup chopped fresh parsley

2 teaspoons Dijon mustard

½ cup plain full-fat Greek yogurt

¼ teaspoon black pepper

¼ teaspoon garlic powder

8 small iceberg lettuce leaves

1. Combine the tuna, shallot, celery, chickpeas, parsley, mustard, yogurt, black pepper, and garlic powder in a medium bowl and mix together.

2. Divide the tuna salad among the lettuce leaves and serve immediately.

 VARIATION: You could serve this with your favorite whole-wheat crackers, or go traditional with whole-wheat bread if the lettuce leaves aren't your style.

Per serving: Calories: 196; Protein: 21g; Total carbs: 21g; Sugars: 6g; Fiber: 5g; Total fat: 4g; Saturated fat: 1g; Cholesterol: 28mg; Sodium: 385mg

Tuna, Avocado, and Cucumber Stuffed Pita

Serves 2 • Prep time: 10 minutes

DAIRY-FREE • UNDER 30 MINUTES

Seafood meals can be hard to fit in when you're short on time. This tuna salad is perfect to eat immediately or pack for lunch. Pack your pita and salad separately and assemble them when you're ready to eat. Save the remaining avocado, cucumber, and onion, and add it to a salad later on in the week.

1 (5-ounce) can tuna packed in olive oil, drained

½ avocado

¼ cup finely chopped cucumber

1 tablespoon finely chopped red onion

1 teaspoon freshly squeezed lemon juice

⅛ teaspoon kosher salt

⅛ teaspoon black pepper

2 whole-wheat pitas, halved and ready to stuff

1. Place the tuna and avocado in a medium bowl and mash together. It doesn't have to be fully combined—pieces of avocado are fine.

2. Add the cucumber, onion, lemon juice, salt, and black pepper and gently mix together.

3. Divide the tuna between the four halves of pita and serve.

 DID YOU KNOW? You don't have to spend a lot of money to get omega-3 fatty acids. Canned tuna is an inexpensive way to get this important nutrient—with little prep work.

Per serving: Calories: 333; Protein: 24g; Total carbs: 36g; Sugars: 2g; Fiber: 6g; Total fat: 11g; Saturated fat: 2g; Cholesterol: 11mg; Sodium: 570mg

Tuna Pasta with Peas and Parmesan

Serves 4 • Prep time: 10 minutes • Cook time: 15 minutes

FEW INGREDIENTS • ONE POT • UNDER 30 MINUTES

If you're looking for a quick and easy way to include more seafood into your diet, look no further than this tuna pasta. The only cooking you have to do is boiling a pot of pasta, making this perfect for those times when you feel like a fuss-free lunch or dinner. I've used orecchiette pasta here, but you can substitute other small shapes like farfalle, fusilli, or penne if that's what you have in the pantry.

2 cups orecchiette pasta

1 cup fresh or frozen peas

2 tablespoons extra-virgin olive oil

¼ teaspoon kosher salt

⅛ teaspoon black pepper

2 (5-ounce) cans tuna packed in olive oil, drained

½ cup freshly grated Parmesan cheese

1. Bring a large pot of water to a boil over medium-high heat. Add the pasta and cook for 9 to 12 minutes, or according to the package directions, until tender. Drain.

2. Transfer the drained pasta to a medium serving bowl. Add the peas, oil, salt, and black pepper, stirring to combine.

3. Add the tuna and Parmesan cheese and stir gently to combine. Serve.

 COOKING TIP: If you use frozen peas, you don't even have to defrost them. Add them to your serving bowl first and then add the hot pasta on top. It's a timesaver, and it keeps you from having to thaw them in a separate dish.

Per serving: Calories: 382; Protein: 28g; Total carbs: 31g; Sugars: 3g; Fiber: 3g; Total fat: 16g; Saturated fat: 4g; Cholesterol: 22mg; Sodium: 555mg

Weeknight Garlic and Lemon Baked Cod

Serves 2 ◆ Prep time: 5 minutes ◆ Cook time: 20 minutes

DAIRY-FREE ◆ FEW INGREDIENTS ◆ GLUTEN-FREE ◆ ONE PAN ◆ UNDER 30 MINUTES

Cod is a versatile white fish with a very neutral flavor that pairs well with many side dishes—plus, it tastes delicious whether fresh or frozen. This dish comes together faster than you can have food delivered to your house.

3 tablespoons extra-virgin olive oil

1 garlic clove, smashed

1 (8-ounce) fresh or thawed from frozen cod fillet, cut into 2 pieces

¼ teaspoon kosher salt

⅛ teaspoon black pepper

1 lemon, sliced into ¼-inch pieces

1. Preheat the oven to 400°F.

2. In a medium oven-safe skillet over medium-low heat, combine the oil and garlic. Cook for 3 to 4 minutes to flavor the oil, then remove and discard the garlic.

3. Season the cod on both sides with the salt and black pepper and place in the skillet with the flavored oil. If the fillets have skin, place them skin-side down. Place the lemon slices around each piece of cod.

4. Turn off the stove and place the skillet in the oven for 12 to 15 minutes, until the fish's interior temperature reads 145°F on a digital thermometer. Serve.

 COOKING TIP: If your oil gets too hot, let it cool before adding the garlic. Garlic burns easily and that will ruin your oil.

Per serving: Calories: 277; Protein: 20g; Total carbs: 3g; Sugars: 1g; Fiber: 1g; Total fat: 21g; Saturated fat: 3g; Cholesterol: 59mg; Sodium: 244mg

Fresh Fish Tacos

Serves 4 • Prep time: 5 minutes • Cook time: 20 minutes

DAIRY-FREE • GLUTEN-FREE • ONE PAN • UNDER 30 MINUTES

This recipe takes the fresh flavors of the Mediterranean and wraps them in a delicious corn tortilla. Call it Tex-Mex/Mediterranean fusion. I've used cod here, but these tacos taste wonderful with many different varieties of fish, including tilapia, red snapper, and salmon. Feel free to use your favorite.

12 ounces cod fillets

½ tablespoon extra-virgin olive oil

¼ teaspoon kosher salt

¼ teaspoon black pepper

12 corn tortillas

1 cup shredded iceberg lettuce

1 avocado, sliced

1 small tomato, chopped

1 small Persian cucumber, chopped

2 tablespoons chopped cilantro leaves (optional)

1 lime, sliced

1. Preheat the oven to 400°F. Line a baking sheet with parchment paper.

2. Place the fish on the prepared baking sheet, drizzle with the oil, and sprinkle with the salt and black pepper. Roast for 20 minutes, or until the fish's interior temperature reads 145°F on a digital thermometer.

3. Flake the fish apart with a fork and add a small amount to each corn tortilla.

4. Assemble the tacos with your toppings of choice: lettuce, avocado, tomato, and cucumber. Garnish with the cilantro (if using) and serve with a piece of lime, for squeezing.

 COOKING TIP: While your fish is cooking, use that time to prepare your taco toppings.

Per serving: Calories: 306; Protein: 20g; Total carbs: 39g; Sugars: 2g; Fiber: 8g; Total fat: 10g; Saturated fat: 1g; Cholesterol: 44mg; Sodium: 186mg

Roasted Cod with Red Pepper Sauce and Capers

Serves 4 • Prep time: 5 minutes • Cook time: 20 minutes

DAIRY-FREE • FEW INGREDIENTS • GLUTEN-FREE • ONE PAN • UNDER 30 MINUTES

With lightning-fast prep, most of the time making this dish is in leaving it to cook in the oven. This gives you the opportunity to either make a side dish on the stovetop, such as Creamed Spinach with Parmesan (page 165), or mix up a quick salad, such as the Classic Greek Salad (page 91).

1 pound fresh or thawed from frozen cod fillets

1 red bell pepper, chopped

1 small onion, chopped

1 garlic clove

1 tablespoon extra-virgin olive oil

½ teaspoon kosher salt

¼ teaspoon black pepper

2 tablespoons capers

1. Preheat the oven to 400°F. Line a baking sheet with parchment paper.

2. Place the cod on one side of the prepared baking sheet and place the bell pepper, onion, and garlic on the other side. Drizzle both the cod and the vegetable mixture with the oil and season with the salt and black pepper. Bake for 20 minutes, or until the fish's interior temperature reads 145°F on a digital thermometer.

3. To make the sauce, transfer the vegetable mixture to a blender and pulse until smooth.

4. Serve the cod with the red pepper sauce and the capers.

 COOKING TIP: With most oven-baked fish dishes, you can use frozen fish, which makes it easier for any night of the week. Fresh cod is inexpensive, but it doesn't last long in the refrigerator. If you can't pick up fish on the same day you want to cook it, your best option is to use frozen.

Per serving: Calories: 134; Protein: 21g; Total carbs: 4g; Sugars: 2g; Fiber: 1g; Total fat: 4g; Saturated fat: 1g; Cholesterol: 59mg; Sodium: 346mg

Pan-Seared Tilapia with Cilantro Gremolata

Serves 4 ◆ Prep time: 5 minutes ◆ Cook time: 10 minutes

DAIRY-FREE ◆ FEW INGREDIENTS ◆ GLUTEN-FREE ◆ UNDER 30 MINUTES

Gremolata is a green sauce from Milan made of chopped herbs, lemon, and garlic. It's paired here with tilapia, the perfect mild fish for those who are new to cooking seafood. It takes on the flavor of herbs and spices easily, which makes it a good choice to pair with just about anything. I love to serve it with a Classic Greek Salad (page 91) or Rosemary Balsamic Roasted Tomatoes and Red Onions (page 163).

FOR THE FISH

½ teaspoon dried oregano

¼ teaspoon garlic powder

¼ teaspoon kosher salt

⅛ teaspoon red pepper flakes

4 (4-ounce) tilapia fillets

2 tablespoons extra-virgin olive oil

FOR THE CILANTRO GREMOLATA

1 garlic clove, peeled

2 tablespoons freshly squeezed lemon juice

2 tablespoons extra-virgin olive oil

¼ cup packed fresh cilantro leaves

¼ teaspoon kosher salt

TO MAKE THE FISH

1. Place the oregano, garlic powder, salt, and red pepper flakes in a small bowl and mix together. Sprinkle the spice mixture over both sides of the tilapia fillets and press gently to stick.

2. Heat a well-seasoned cast-iron or nonstick skillet over medium heat and add the oil. Wait 2 minutes for the oil to heat up, then add the tilapia fillets.

3. Cook for about 4 minutes on one side, then flip and cook for 4 minutes on the other side, or until the fish's interior temperature reads 145°F on a digital thermometer.

TO MAKE THE CILANTRO GREMOLATA

4. Combine the garlic, lemon juice, oil, cilantro, and salt in a blender and pulse until smooth.

5. Serve each tilapia fillet with 1 tablespoon of gremolata drizzled on top.

❖ **COOKING TIP:** Try to flip your fish only once during the cooking process. Tilapia is delicate and too much flipping can cause it to break apart.

Per serving: Calories: 232; Protein: 23g; Total carbs: 1g; Sugars: <1g; Fiber: <1g; Total fat: 16g; Saturated fat: 3g; Cholesterol: 57mg; Sodium: 200mg

Tomato Basil Tilapia in Olive Oil

Serves 4 • Prep time: 5 minutes • Cook time: 20 minutes

DAIRY-FREE • FEW INGREDIENTS • GLUTEN-FREE • ONE PAN • UNDER 30 MINUTES

This recipe is essentially a sheet pan dinner done in a skillet. I love the ease of this dish, because there is minimal prep work before getting it into the oven. Use a skillet large enough to fit everything without overcrowding, but if you don't have one, a sheet pan works, too.

3 tablespoons extra-virgin olive oil, divided

4 (4-ounce) tilapia fillets

2 cups cherry tomatoes

¼ teaspoon kosher salt

¼ teaspoon black pepper

¼ cup shredded fresh basil

1. Preheat the oven to 400°F.

2. In a large oven-proof skillet, warm 2 tablespoons of oil until just shimmering. Add the fish, place the tomatoes around them, sprinkle with the salt and black pepper, and drizzle the remaining 1 tablespoon of oil over all.

3. Bake for 20 minutes, or until the fish's interior temperature reads 145°F on a digital thermometer.

4. Garnish with the basil and serve.

 VARIATION: If roasted tomatoes aren't your favorite, you can roast the tilapia alone and then make a quick fresh tomato and basil side salad instead.

Per serving: Calories: 214; Protein: 24g; Total carbs: 3g; Sugars: 1g; Fiber: 1g; Total fat: 12g; Saturated fat: 2g; Cholesterol: 57mg; Sodium: 134mg

Flounder with Tomato and Spinach Sauce

Serves 4 ✦ Prep time: 5 minutes ✦ Cook time: 25 minutes
GLUTEN-FREE

In the mid-1600s, Catherine de' Medici, the queen consort of King Henry II and a native of Florence, introduced spinach dishes to the French court and proclaimed them to be "Florentine." This Florentine-style dish pairs roasted fish with a lightly creamed tomato and spinach sauce. Any white fish works beautifully here if you don't care for flounder.

4 (4-ounce) flounder fillets

3 tablespoons extra-virgin olive oil, divided

¼ teaspoon kosher salt

¼ teaspoon black pepper

1 small onion, finely chopped

2 garlic cloves, minced

1 (10-ounce) bag baby spinach

1 (15-ounce) can fire-roasted tomatoes

⅓ cup heavy cream

⅛ teaspoon red pepper flakes

1. Preheat the oven to 400°F. Line a baking sheet with aluminum foil.

2. Place the flounder fillets on the prepared baking sheet, drizzle with 1 tablespoon of oil, and season with the salt and black pepper. Roast the fish for 20 minutes, or until it breaks off easily with a fork and the interior temperature reads 145°F on a digital thermometer.

3. While the fish is cooking, in a large skillet over medium-high heat, combine the remaining 2 tablespoons of oil and the onion. Sauté for 3 to 4 minutes, until the onion is translucent. Add the garlic, spinach, and tomatoes and sauté for 10 to 15 minutes, or until all the spinach has wilted down and almost all the liquid has evaporated. Turn the heat to low and stir in the heavy cream.

4. Nestle the cooked fish into the sauce and sprinkle with the red pepper flakes. Turn off the heat and let the fish rest in the mixture for 3 to 4 minutes to absorb the flavors of the sauce. Serve.

 SUBSTITUTION TIP: If you don't have fresh spinach, you could substitute 10 ounces of frozen spinach. Thaw it and squeeze all the water out before adding it to the skillet.

Per serving: Calories: 277; Protein: 27g; Total carbs: 13g; Sugars: 6g; Fiber: 4g; Total fat: 19g; Saturated fat: 6g; Cholesterol: 68mg; Sodium: 454mg

Salmon Patties

Serves 4 ◆ Prep time: 10 minutes ◆ Cook time: 15 minutes

UNDER 30 MINUTES

If you're easing yourself into eating more seafood, salmon patties are a recipe you should try. If you want to pair them with a sauce, the tzatziki recipe on page 85 is a perfect accompaniment. Reheat leftover salmon patties in the oven or in a toaster oven to get them crispy again.

1 pound canned salmon, salmon packets, or cooked leftover salmon

1 large egg

½ cup Italian seasoned breadcrumbs

¼ cup plain full-fat Greek yogurt

2 teaspoons Dijon mustard

2 teaspoons chopped fresh dill

2 tablespoons extra-virgin olive oil

1. Place the salmon in a medium bowl and break it apart with a fork. Add the egg, breadcrumbs, yogurt, mustard, and dill and gently stir until it just comes together.

2. Scoop up ¼ cup of the mixture with your hands and form it into a patty. Repeat this process until the mixture is gone. You should have 12 patties.

3. In a medium skillet over medium heat, heat the oil until it shimmers.

4. One by one, carefully place the patties in the hot oil with some space between them. If you run out of room in the skillet, work in batches.

5. Cook for 3 to 4 minutes on one side, then flip and cook for another 3 minutes on the other side. Both the sides should be golden brown.

6. Let the salmon patties rest on a paper towel for 1 to 2 minutes to absorb the excess oil. Serve warm.

 VARIATION: If you have cans of tuna in the pantry, use those instead of the salmon. You could even use flavored tuna and really change up this recipe each time.

Per serving: Calories: 306; Protein: 31g; Total carbs: 11g; Sugars: 2g; Fiber: 1g; Total fat: 15g; Saturated fat: 3g; Cholesterol: 138mg; Sodium: 712mg

Pesto Salmon with Pine Nuts and Lemon

Serves 4 • Prep time: 5 minutes • Cook time: 20 minutes

FEW INGREDIENTS • GLUTEN-FREE • ONE PAN • UNDER 30 MINUTES

Salmon is easy to prepare and cooks quickly, making it perfect for weeknight dinners. It is an ideal fish for the Mediterranean diet due to its high amounts of healthy omega-3 fatty acids and vitamin D.

Nonstick cooking spray

1 pound skin-on salmon fillet, or 4 (4-ounce) fillets

⅓ cup basil pesto

¼ cup pine nuts

1 lemon, cut into 4 wedges

1. Preheat the oven to 400°F. Line a baking sheet with aluminum foil and spray the foil with nonstick cooking spray.

2. Place the salmon fillets, skin-side down, on the prepared baking sheet. Spread the pesto evenly on the salmon.

3. Bake for 20 minutes, or until the salmon easily flakes with a fork and the interior temperature reads 145°F on a digital thermometer.

4. Sprinkle 1 tablespoon of pine nuts on each portion and squeeze a lemon wedge over the top before serving.

 VARIATION: If you have an indoor or outdoor grill, you can slide the foil directly onto the grill and cook over high heat for the same amount of time.

Per serving: Calories: 256; Protein: 24g; Total carbs: 3g; Sugars: 1g; Fiber: 1g; Total fat: 17g; Saturated fat: 3g; Cholesterol: 66mg; Sodium: 352mg

Salmon and Broccoli with Lemon Dill Sauce

Serves 4 ◆ Prep time: 5 minutes ◆ Cook time: 20 minutes

DAIRY-FREE ◆ FEW INGREDIENTS ◆ GLUTEN-FREE ◆ ONE PAN ◆ UNDER 30 MINUTES

Sheet pan dinners are perfect for busy weeknights, and salmon is the perfect fish for sheet pans. It cooks fast, but not too fast, so you can get vegetables cooked in the same amount of time. Make the lemon dill sauce while the salmon is cooking to save even more time.

FOR THE FISH

1 pound salmon fillet, cut into 4 pieces

1 large broccoli crown, cut into florets

3 tablespoons extra-virgin olive oil, divided

¾ teaspoon kosher salt

¼ teaspoon black pepper

FOR THE LEMON DILL SAUCE

1 tablespoon extra-virgin olive oil

Juice of 1 lemon

2 tablespoons chopped fresh dill

½ teaspoon kosher salt

⅛ teaspoon black pepper

TO MAKE THE FISH

1. Preheat the oven to 400°F. Line baking sheet with parchment paper.

2. Place salmon in the middle of the prepared baking sheet and arrange the broccoli around it. Toss the broccoli with 2 tablespoons of oil, then drizzle the remaining 1 tablespoon of oil on the salmon. Sprinkle the salt and black pepper over the salmon and broccoli.

3. Bake for 20 minutes, or until the salmon breaks apart easily with a fork and the interior temperature reads 145°F on a digital thermometer.

TO MAKE THE LEMON DILL SAUCE

4. Combine the oil, lemon juice, dill, salt, and black pepper in a small covered container and shake to mix.

5. Plate the salmon and broccoli and drizzle the lemon dill sauce on top. Serve.

Per serving: Calories: 265; Protein: 23g; Total carbs: 4g; Sugars: 3g; Fiber: 1g; Total fat: 18g; Saturated fat: 3g; Cholesterol: 55mg; Sodium: 533mg

Spaghetti Aglio e Olio with Shrimp

Serves 4 ✦ Prep time: 10 minutes ✦ Cook time: 15 minutes
UNDER 30 MINUTES

This simple Italian dish translates as "spaghetti with garlic and oil." Shrimp is quick cooking and adds a perfect punch of protein to this dish without any fuss. If you want to make this meal even healthier, substitute a whole-wheat or bean pasta, or even zucchini noodles.

8 ounces spaghetti pasta

¼ cup, plus 2 tablespoons extra-virgin olive oil, divided

12 ounces fresh or thawed from frozen shrimp, peeled, deveined, and tails removed

3 garlic cloves, minced

½ teaspoon kosher salt

¼ teaspoon black pepper

½ cup freshly grated Parmesan cheese

¼ teaspoon red pepper flakes

1 lemon, cut into 4 wedges

2 tablespoons minced fresh parsley or thinly sliced scallions

1. Bring a large pot of water to boil over medium-high heat. Add the pasta and cook for 8 to 12 minutes, or according to the package directions, until tender. Drain and set aside.

2. While the pasta is cooking, warm ¼ cup of oil in a large skillet over medium heat until just shimmering. Add the shrimp, garlic, salt, and black pepper. Cook for about 3 minutes on each side, until the shrimp is pink.

3. Turn the heat to low. Add the cooked pasta and Parmesan cheese and toss. Drizzle the remaining 2 tablespoons of oil and the red pepper flakes over the top and toss again.

4. Garnish each serving with a lemon wedge and the parsley.

 COOKING TIP: This is the perfect dish to use with frozen shrimp. It also makes a perfect last-minute dish.

Per serving: Calories: 520; Protein: 25g; Total carbs: 46g; Sugars: 2g; Fiber: 3g; Total fat: 27g; Saturated fat: 5g; Cholesterol: 192mg; Sodium: 1033mg

Garlic Shrimp with Polenta

Serves 4 • Prep time: 10 minutes, plus 1 hour to marinate • Cook time: 35 minutes

GLUTEN-FREE

Polenta is a creamy cornmeal dish popular in Italy. Polenta grains are a coarse grind of cornmeal that make for an excellent gluten-free source of fiber and protein. This is a favorite in my house and a great way to get more seafood in your week.

FOR THE SHRIMP

2 tablespoons extra-virgin olive oil

2 garlic cloves, minced

1 tablespoon chopped fresh parsley

¼ teaspoon kosher salt

¼ teaspoon black pepper

1 pound fresh or thawed from frozen shrimp, peeled, deveined, and tails removed

FOR THE POLENTA

1 tablespoon extra-virgin olive oil

1 small onion, finely chopped

2 garlic cloves, minced

1 cup polenta

¼ teaspoon kosher salt

4 cups low-sodium chicken stock or vegetable broth

½ cup freshly grated Parmesan cheese

2 tablespoons chopped fresh parsley

TO MAKE THE SHRIMP

1. In a covered container or zip-top bag, mix together the oil, garlic, parsley, salt, and black pepper. Add the shrimp and let them marinate in the refrigerator for 1 hour.

TO MAKE THE POLENTA

2. Heat a medium Dutch oven or deep skillet over medium heat. Add the oil, onion, and garlic and sauté for 2 minutes, until they are only slightly cooked. Add the polenta and salt and stir to combine.

3. Add the stock, 1 cup at a time, stirring continuously for 25 minutes, until the polenta has absorbed all the liquid. Remove from the heat, stir in the Parmesan cheese, and let sit for 5 minutes.

4. Remove the shrimp from the marinade. In a medium skillet over medium-high heat, sauté the shrimp for 2 minutes, until one side is pink, then turn them over and cook for 2 minutes, until the other side is pink.

5. Divide the polenta and shrimp among four plates and garnish with the parsley. Serve.

❖ **COOKING TIP:** You can get this dish on the table faster by starting the polenta 30 minutes into the marinating time.

Per serving: Calories: 404; Protein: 27g; Total carbs: 37g; Sugars: 1g; Fiber: 2g; Total fat: 18g; Saturated fat: 4g; Cholesterol: 254mg; Sodium: 1291mg

Seafood Paella

Serves 4 ◆ Prep time: 5 minutes ◆ Cook time: 1 hour

DAIRY-FREE ◆ GLUTEN-FREE ◆ ONE PAN

A prized dish in Spanish cuisine, paella is traditionally made with chicken and rabbit, but it lends itself wonderfully to seafood such as shrimp, mussels, and calamari. At its heart is a slowly simmered aromatic base known as a *sofrito*, a savory-sweet blend of tomatoes, onions, garlic, and bell pepper. Modify this basic paella recipe as you wish. Leave the seafood out and add fresh veggies, or add cooked chicken at the very end.

3 tablespoons extra-virgin olive oil

1 tomato, chopped

1 small onion, chopped

1 small green bell pepper, chopped

2 garlic cloves, minced

2½ cups low-sodium seafood or chicken stock, or vegetable broth

½ teaspoon kosher salt

½ teaspoon ground turmeric

½ teaspoon paprika

1 cup short-grain rice, such as bomba or arborio

12 ounces mixed seafood, such as shrimp, mussels, and/or calamari

1. In a large, shallow cast-iron or enamel skillet, or a paella pan, heat the oil over medium-low heat until it shimmers. Add the tomato, onion, bell pepper, and garlic and cook for 20 to 25 minutes, stirring every 5 minutes.

2. Add the stock, salt, turmeric, and paprika and bring to a boil. Add the rice and stir once to ensure the rice is evenly coating the bottom of the pan. Turn the heat to low and simmer, uncovered, for 15 minutes. Do not stir again.

3. Add the seafood on top of the rice and simmer for another 10 minutes, flipping the seafood once halfway through the cooking time, or until it is cooked through. Serve.

❖ **COOKING TIP:** Resist the urge to stir the paella once you add the rice, so a deliciously crispy crust can form on its underside. Instead, rotate the pan every few minutes while the rice is cooking. This will ensure even cooking and avoid having hard pieces of rice on the edges of the pan.

Per serving: Calories: 347; Protein: 16g; Total carbs: 46g; Sugars: 3g; Fiber: 3g; Total fat: 12g; Saturated fat: 2g; Cholesterol: 180mg; Sodium: 858mg

Poultry and Meat Mains

Creamy Pesto Chicken and Arugula

Serves 4 • Prep time: 10 minutes

GLUTEN-FREE • ONE POT • UNDER 30 MINUTES

This deliciously creamy chicken dish uses ingredients common throughout this book, so it's a great option to use up any extra pesto, yogurt, or sun-dried tomatoes you have in the refrigerator. If you are making this for the meal plan and are using some for leftovers, pack up the chicken salad and the arugula separately and combine them when you are ready to eat.

1 avocado, halved, pitted, and peeled

⅓ cup basil pesto

2 tablespoons plain full-fat Greek yogurt

4 cups shredded rotisserie chicken (about 1 pound)

8 cups arugula

4 tablespoons sliced sun-dried tomatoes in oil

1. In a medium bowl, mash the avocado until it's smooth. Add the pesto and yogurt and mix until they're fully combined. Add the chicken and mix together.

2. Divide the arugula among four serving bowls. Place the chicken salad on top and garnish with the sun-dried tomatoes. Serve.

 COOKING TIP: If you don't have rotisserie chicken, roast 1 pound of boneless, skinless chicken breasts instead. Preheat the oven to 375°F. Place the chicken on a foil-lined baking sheet, drizzle with ½ tablespoon of olive oil, ¼ teaspoon of kosher salt, and ⅛ teaspoon of black pepper. Roast for 30 to 35 minutes, depending on the size, until the internal temperature is 165°F. You can cook the chicken up to three days in advance.

Per serving: Calories: 408; Protein: 30g; Total carbs: 9g; Sugars: 2g; Fiber: 4g; Total fat: 28g; Saturated fat: 6g; Cholesterol: 113mg; Sodium: 610mg

Chicken Burger Lettuce Wraps

Serves 4 ◆ Prep time: 10 minutes ◆ Cook time: 15 minutes

GLUTEN-FREE ◆ UNDER 30 MINUTES

Adapting the Mediterranean diet to the foods you already enjoy is what will make it even more fun and sustainable. Everyone loves a good burger, and this recipe brings in some Greek flavors while staying relatively low in calories by substituting a lettuce wrap for the bun.

4 big iceberg or Bibb lettuce leaves

2 tablespoons extra-virgin olive oil, divided

2 tablespoons finely chopped red onion

2 big handfuls baby spinach

1 garlic clove, minced

1 pound ground chicken

½ teaspoon kosher salt

¼ teaspoon black pepper

3 ounces crumbled feta cheese

OPTIONAL TOPPINGS

Tzatziki (page 85)

Diced tomatoes

Diced cucumbers

Sliced red onion

1. Wash the lettuce leaves and set them on a clean towel to dry.

2. In a skillet over medium heat, combine 1 tablespoon of oil, the onion, spinach, and garlic. Sauté for 3 minutes, until the spinach is wilted, stirring once or twice so the garlic doesn't burn.

3. Transfer the sautéed vegetables to a large bowl and add the chicken, salt, and black pepper. Combine the mixture with a spoon or your hands until it's well mixed. When you are ready to start forming your burgers, add the crumbled feta to the mixture and carefully mix one more time with your hands. Form the chicken into four burgers.

4. In the same skillet, add the remaining 1 tablespoon of oil and heat over medium-high heat until just shimmering. Place the burgers in the skillet and cook without flipping for 5 to 6 minutes, until they start to look white all over. Flip them over and cook the other side cook for 4 to 5 minutes, or until their internal temperature reads 165°F on a digital thermometer.

5. Wrap the burgers in the lettuce leaves and serve with the toppings (if using).

 SUBSTITUTION TIP: If you don't have or can't find ground chicken, ground turkey or even lean ground beef works just as well.

Per serving: Calories: 285; Protein: 23g; Total carbs: 2g; Sugars: 1g; Fiber: <1g; Total fat: 21g; Saturated fat: 6g; Cholesterol: 116mg; Sodium: 458mg

Italian Chicken Sausage and Peppers Skillet

Serves 4 ◆ Prep time: 5 minutes ◆ Cook time: 20 minutes

DAIRY-FREE ◆ GLUTEN-FREE ◆ ONE PAN ◆ UNDER 30 MINUTES

A classic Italian sausage and peppers recipe is a little outside the weight-loss-friendly zone, but substituting chicken sausage cuts down saturated fat and calories by half. If you want to round out this dish to make a meal, it's great served alongside the Weeknight Garden Salad with Vinaigrette (page 90).

2 tablespoons extra-virgin olive oil

1 large red bell pepper, sliced

1 large green bell pepper, sliced

2 onions, sliced

8 ounces white button mushrooms, sliced

4 cooked Italian chicken sausage links, sliced

¼ teaspoon kosher salt (optional)

1 tablespoon chopped fresh cilantro

1. In a large skillet over medium heat, heat the oil until it shimmers. Add the red and green bell peppers, onion, and mushrooms and sauté for 10 minutes, until the peppers are soft.

2. Add the sausage and sauté for 5 to 7 minutes, until the sausage is heated through and lightly browned.

3. Season with the salt (if using) and garnish with the cilantro before serving.

 VARIATION: This is a great dish to clear out the veggie drawer with: zucchini, eggplant, and other types of bell peppers can all be added.

Per serving: Calories: 256; Protein: 20g; Total carbs: 12g; Sugars: 7g; Fiber: 4g; Total fat: 15g; Saturated fat: 4g; Cholesterol: 55mg; Sodium: 599m

Slow-Roasted Chicken and Chickpea Stew

Serves 4 • Prep time: 10 minutes • Cook time: 3 hours

DAIRY-FREE • ONE POT

The long cook time is well worth it for this stew. The slow roasting produces beautifully tender meat and vegetables in a richly flavored sauce. The prep can be done in 10 minutes flat, so you can put it in the oven and tend to other things around the home. This stew embodies the Mediterranean approach of taking your time with food, rather than always opting for the fastest way to get things done.

½ red onion, chopped

1 (15-ounce) can chickpeas, with their liquid

1 (15-ounce) can fire-roasted tomatoes

2 tablespoons extra-virgin olive oil

2 tablespoons all-purpose flour

Juice of 1 lemon

1 garlic clove, grated

1 teaspoon ground cumin

½ teaspoon ground turmeric

1 pound boneless, skinless chicken breasts

1. Preheat the oven to 300°F.

2. Add the onion, chickpeas and their liquid, tomatoes, oil, flour, lemon juice, garlic, cumin, and turmeric, in that order, to a large Dutch oven or baking dish with a lid. Stir the ingredients together and nestle the chicken on top. Cover.

3. Roast for 3 hours, or until the chicken's internal temperature reads 165°F on a digital thermometer.

4. Remove from the oven. While still in the pot, use two forks to break apart the chicken into large pieces.

5. Place the cover back on the pot and let the stew rest for 10 minutes before serving.

 VARIATION: This can be made in a slow cooker, if you have one. Add everything to the slow cooker and cook on high for 4 hours.

Per serving: Calories: 343; Protein: 32g; Total carbs: 29g; Sugars: 8g; Fiber: 7g; Total fat: 12g; Saturated fat: 2g; Cholesterol: 80mg; Sodium: 454mg

Chicken Gyro Bowl

Serves 4 • Prep time: 5 minutes • Cook time: 35 minutes
GLUTEN-FREE

This is one of my favorite weekday lunches. I always have most of these ingredients on hand. Even if it's just for me, I like to roast all the chicken at once and eat this all week.

1 pound boneless, skinless chicken breasts

1 tablespoon, plus 4 teaspoons extra-virgin olive oil, divided

¼ teaspoon kosher salt

¼ teaspoon black pepper

1 (10-ounce) bag field greens

1 large tomato, chopped

½ small red onion, thinly sliced

1 Persian cucumber, chopped

1 cup plain full-fat Greek yogurt

1 tablespoon freshly squeezed lemon juice

2 tablespoons chopped fresh dill (optional)

2 ounces crumbled feta cheese

1. Preheat the oven to 375°F. Line a baking sheet with aluminum foil.

2. Place the chicken on the prepared baking sheet, drizzle with 1 tablespoon of oil, and sprinkle with the salt and black pepper. Roast for 30 to 35 minutes, or until the chicken's internal temperature reads 165°F on a digital thermometer. Remove from the oven and let rest for 5 minutes before slicing the chicken into thin strips.

3. In each serving bowl, place some greens and add the tomato, red onion, cucumber, and cooked chicken.

4. In a separate small bowl, combine the yogurt, lemon juice, and dill (if using). Top each serving with ¼ cup of yogurt sauce, the feta, and 1 teaspoon of the remaining oil.

 VARIATION: If you need a little something extra with this meal, add a small whole-wheat pita to each bowl and use it to scoop everything together.

Per serving: Calories: 327; Protein: 35g; Total carbs: 9g; Sugars: 5g; Fiber: 3g; Total fat: 18g; Saturated fat: 6g; Cholesterol: 106mg; Sodium: 458mg

Creamy Sun-Dried Tomato Chicken

Serves 4 ◆ Prep time: 5 minutes ◆ Cook time: 20 minutes

FEW INGREDIENTS ◆ GLUTEN-FREE ◆ ONE PAN ◆ UNDER 30 MINUTES

You might be surprised to see a recipe title with the word "creamy" in a weight-loss book, but you need only very small amounts of cream to create big flavor. It's not too much, but it pairs beautifully with the intense flavor of the sun-dried tomatoes. I make this with half cream and half milk to create my own half-and-half.

3 tablespoons extra-virgin olive oil

½ teaspoon kosher salt

½ teaspoon Italian seasoning

1 pound boneless, skinless chicken breasts, either pounded gently or cut into ½-inch-thick cutlets

⅓ cup chopped sun-dried tomatoes in oil

¼ cup heavy cream

¼ cup 2% milk

1. In a medium skillet, heat the oil over medium-high heat until it shimmers. Sprinkle the salt and Italian seasoning over the chicken and place it in the skillet. Cook for 4 to 5 minutes on each side, until the chicken's internal temperature reads 165°F on a digital thermometer.

2. Turn the heat down to medium and add the sun-dried tomatoes, cream, and milk. Simmer the cream mixture for 2 to 3 minutes, until thickened, then remove from the heat.

3. Let the chicken rest for 3 minutes before serving.

 COOKING TIP: Pair this with Honey-Roasted Carrots (page 167) and Weeknight Garden Salad with Vinaigrette (page 90). You can prep the carrots and get them in the oven before you start the main dish, and assemble the salad and dressing while the chicken is cooking on the stovetop.

Per serving: Calories: 297; Protein: 26g; Total carbs: 3g; Sugars: 3g; Fiber: 1g; Total fat: 20g; Saturated fat: 6g; Cholesterol: 98mg; Sodium: 226mg

Tuscan Chicken and Orzo Skillet

Serves 4 • Prep time: 5 minutes • Cook time: 25 minutes

DAIRY-FREE • ONE PAN

I love an all-in-one meal, and this Tuscan dish certainly fits the bill with the chicken, vegetables, and pasta all cooking together in a single skillet. Make good use of your time when the meat is cooking to prep the veggies.

4 tablespoons extra-virgin olive oil, divided

1 pound boneless, skinless chicken breasts, cut into ½-inch cubes

½ teaspoon kosher salt, divided

¼ teaspoon black pepper

1 small yellow bell pepper, chopped

1 small onion, chopped

2 garlic cloves, minced

1 (8-ounce) package frozen spinach, thawed (not drained)

1 (15-ounce) can fire-roasted tomatoes

1 cup orzo pasta

1 cup water

2 teaspoons Italian seasoning

¼ cup chopped green olives

1 tablespoon red wine vinegar

1. In a large skillet, heat 2 tablespoons of oil over medium-high heat until just shimmering. Add the chicken, ¼ teaspoon of salt, and the black pepper and cook for 8 to 10 minutes, until the chicken is lightly browned on all sides and the internal temperature reads 165°F on a digital thermometer. Transfer the chicken to a plate.

2. In the same skillet, add the remaining 2 tablespoons of oil, the bell pepper, and onion and sauté for 3 minutes. Add the garlic and sauté for 1 minute.

3. Add the spinach, tomatoes, orzo, water, Italian seasoning, and remaining ¼ teaspoon of salt. Cover, reduce the heat to low, and simmer for 8 minutes, or until the orzo is tender.

4. Add the olives, vinegar, and cooked chicken, stirring to combine before serving.

 VARIATION: The orzo adds substance if you're cooking for a family. You can cut calories in your meal even more if you leave it out. This dish can also be stretched by adding more chicken and keeping the orzo in.

Per serving: Calories: 498; Protein: 35g; Total carbs: 48g; Sugars: 9g; Fiber: 11g; Total fat: 19g; Saturated fat: 3g; Cholesterol: 80mg; Sodium: 644mg

Spanish-Style Meatballs in Tomato Sauce

Serves 4 ◆ Prep time: 10 minutes ◆ Cook time: 25 minutes

DAIRY-FREE

Beef is not eaten in large amounts in Mediterranean cuisine, but meatballs are very traditional across southern Europe. Typically, they are made with a combination of beef, pork, and/or lamb. That gets expensive and can significantly increase calories. These meatballs use extra-lean ground beef, which can get dry when cooked in the oven. Cooking them on the stovetop in a sauce helps keep them juicy.

¼ cup finely chopped red onion

2 garlic cloves, minced

⅓ cup seasoned breadcrumbs

1 large egg

½ teaspoon smoked paprika

1 pound extra-lean (97%) ground beef

2 tablespoons extra-virgin olive oil

3 cups marinara sauce

1. In a medium bowl, combine the onion, garlic, breadcrumbs, egg, paprika, and beef and mix together with a strong spoon or your hands. Form into 12 meatballs.

2. Heat the oil in a medium skillet over medium-high heat until it shimmers. Add the meatballs and cook, turning every minute, for 6 minutes, or until brown on all sides. (They will not be fully cooked at this point.)

3. Add the marinara sauce, turn the heat to low, and simmer for 20 minutes, or until the meatballs' internal temperature reads 155°F on a digital thermometer. Serve.

 SUBSTITUTION TIP: If you don't have seasoned breadcrumbs, use regular and add ¼ teaspoon of kosher salt to the meatball mixture. Choose a brand of marinara sauce with no added sugar, or use crushed tomatoes instead and add a pinch of salt and pepper. And finally, if you don't have or don't like the taste of smoked paprika, use regular paprika.

Per serving (3 meatballs): Calories: 416; Protein: 36g; Total carbs: 30g; Sugars: 16g; Fiber: 4g; Total fat: 18g; Saturated fat: 5g; Cholesterol: 141mg; Sodium: 920mg

Beef and Hummus Pitas

Serves 4 ◆ Prep time: 10 minutes ◆ Cook time: 15 minutes

DAIRY-FREE ◆ ONE PAN ◆ UNDER 30 MINUTES

This dish checks off all the boxes: It's easy to cook, has an intense flavor, and packs well for leftovers. You don't have to make your own hummus, but if you have leftover Roasted Garlic Hummus (page 84), that works well. If you are saving some of this for lunch, pack the meat, hummus, and pita separately and assemble it when you're ready to eat.

2 tablespoons extra-virgin olive oil

1 small onion, chopped

2 garlic cloves, minced

1 teaspoon ground cumin

½ teaspoon ground coriander

½ teaspoon kosher salt

¼ teaspoon black pepper

¼ teaspoon ground cinnamon

1 pound extra-lean (97%) ground beef or ground turkey

¼ cup raisins

¼ cup pine nuts

4 (4-inch) whole-wheat pita rounds, halved

½ cup hummus

1. In a medium skillet over medium heat, combine the oil and onion and sauté for 3 to 4 minutes, until the onion is translucent. Add the garlic, cumin, coriander, salt, black pepper, and cinnamon, stirring to combine.

2. Add the beef and break it apart with a wooden spoon. Cook for 7 to 8 minutes, until the beef is brown and cooked through. Stir in the raisins and pine nuts.

3. In each pita half, place 1 tablespoon of hummus and ¼ cup of the meat mixture. Serve.

 COOKING TIP: If you use beef with a higher fat content, cook it first and drain any excess grease, then add it into the dish in step 2 and stir in the raisins and pine nuts right away.

Per serving: Calories: 433; Protein: 31g; Total carbs: 31g; Sugars: 8g; Fiber: 5g; Total fat: 21g; Saturated fat: 5g; Cholesterol: 68mg; Sodium: 473mg

Greek-Style Stuffed Tomatoes

Serves 4 ◆ Prep time: 25 minutes ◆ Cook time: 50 minutes

GLUTEN-FREE

This recipe went through a few changes before I landed on the perfect flavor combo to please my trusted recipe testers—my children! If you can't find large tomatoes, eight medium tomatoes work well, too. If you need to feed a crowd, this recipe doubles well to fit in a larger baking dish with the same cooking time.

4 large tomatoes

½ pound extra-lean (97%) ground beef

2 tablespoons extra-virgin olive oil

1 small onion, chopped

2 garlic cloves, minced

1 carrot, finely grated

1 (10-ounce) bag baby spinach, chopped

½ teaspoon dried oregano

½ teaspoon kosher salt

4 ounces crumbled feta cheese

1. Preheat the oven to 400°F. Position a rack in the bottom of the oven.

2. Cut the tops off the tomatoes and scoop out the insides with a spoon. Reserve the flesh and liquid in a bowl.

3. Heat a skillet over medium-high heat and cook the beef, breaking it apart with a wooden spoon, for 7 minutes, until brown and cooked through. Transfer the beef to a colander and drain any grease.

4. In the same skillet over medium heat, heat the oil until it shimmers. Add the reserved tomato flesh and liquid, onion, garlic, carrot, spinach, oregano, and salt. Simmer for 5 to 10 minutes, or until most but not all the liquid has cooked out.

5. Remove from the heat, then stir the beef back in. Add the feta and gently stir to combine.

6. Divide the mixture evenly among the tomatoes and stuff them until they are overfilled (they will cook down).

7. Place the tomatoes in a medium baking dish (they should fit snugly) and bake for 30 minutes. Serve.

 VARIATION: You can vary this recipe using ground turkey or cooked chicken, or you could make it a vegetarian dish by using quinoa or lentils instead of meat.

Per serving: Calories: 268; Protein: 21g; Total carbs: 14g; Sugars: 8g; Fiber: 5g; Total fat: 15g; Saturated fat: 6g; Cholesterol: 59mg; Sodium: 577mg

Moroccan-Inspired Beef with Couscous

Serves 4 ◆ Prep time: 5 minutes ◆ Cook time: 20 minutes

DAIRY-FREE ◆ UNDER 30 MINUTES

This delicious, hearty beef and couscous dish will infuse your kitchen with fragrant spices common in Moroccan cooking. The touch of cinnamon brings a subtle undertone of sweetness that marries wonderfully with the more dominant savory flavors. Feel free to top it with fresh cilantro, a dollop of Greek yogurt, and even slivered almonds. If you are using ground beef with a higher fat content, cook it first to drain the extra grease, and add it back in after the carrots and onions are cooked.

1 cup water (or according to couscous package directions)

1 cup couscous

2 tablespoons extra-virgin olive oil

2 carrots, finely chopped

1 onion, finely chopped

1 garlic clove, minced

1 pound extra-lean (97%) ground beef

½ teaspoon kosher salt

1 teaspoon ground cinnamon

1 teaspoon ground turmeric

1 teaspoon ground coriander

1 teaspoon ground cumin

½ teaspoon black pepper

2 tablespoons tomato paste

½ cup water

1. Cook the couscous according to the package directions. Typically this means bringing the water to a boil over medium-high heat, then removing it from the heat. Immediately add the couscous, cover, and let sit for 10 minutes, or until the liquid is absorbed and the couscous is tender. Set aside.

2. In a medium skillet over medium-high heat, add the oil, carrots, and onion and sauté for 3 to 4 minutes, until the onion is translucent. Add the garlic and the beef and cook, breaking it up with a wooden spoon, for 7 to 8 minutes, until the beef is brown and cooked through.

3. Add the salt, cinnamon, turmeric, coriander, cumin, and black pepper, stirring to combine. Add the tomato paste and water, stirring to combine.

4. Divide the couscous among four bowls and serve the beef on top.

❖ **DID YOU KNOW?** Turmeric is an antioxidant that has been studied extensively for its anti-inflammatory properties. Black pepper helps your body absorb turmeric, so be sure to use them together when cooking.

Per serving: Calories: 397; Protein: 32g; Total carbs: 42g; Sugars: 5g; Fiber: 4g; Total fat: 11g; Saturated fat: 3g; Cholesterol: 68mg; Sodium: 248mg

Parmesan and Chive
Pork Loin Chops

Serves 4 ◆ Prep time: 5 minutes ◆ Cook time: 15 minutes

FEW INGREDIENTS ◆ GLUTEN-FREE ◆ ONE PAN ◆ UNDER 30 MINUTES

There are times when you need a quick dinner. But why waste time sitting in a drive-thru when you can cook yourself a delicious healthy meal in 20 minutes? I like to serve this with the Classic Greek Salad (page 91).

2 tablespoons extra-virgin olive oil

1 garlic clove, smashed

1 pound boneless pork loin chops, about ½-inch thick

½ teaspoon Italian seasoning

½ teaspoon kosher salt

¼ cup freshly grated Parmesan cheese

2 tablespoons chopped fresh chives

1. Heat the oil in a large skillet over medium-high heat until it shimmers. Add the garlic and cook, flipping frequently, for 1 to 2 minutes, until it starts to soften. Remove it from the pan.

2. Season both sides of the pork chops with the Italian seasoning and salt and place them in the hot skillet. Cook on one side for 5 minutes, then flip to the other side and cook for 4 to 5 minutes, until both sides of the pork chops are lightly golden brown and the internal temperature reads 145°F on a digital thermometer.

3. When serving each chop, add 1 tablespoon of Parmesan cheese and ½ tablespoon chives. If there are pan juices, drizzle a small amount on each chop.

 DID YOU KNOW? While the Mediterranean diet allows for some red meat each month, you should always choose healthy cuts. For pork, these include loin chops, tenderloin, and sirloin roast. Avoid bacon and other cuts that are high in saturated fats.

Per serving: Calories: 232; Protein: 27g; Total carbs: 1g; Sugars: 0g; Fiber: <1g; Total fat: 12g; Saturated fat: 3g; Cholesterol: 80mg; Sodium: 309mg

Pork Tenderloin with Caramelized Mushrooms

Serves 4 ♦ Prep time: 5 minutes ♦ Cook time: 40 minutes

FEW INGREDIENTS

Pork tenderloin is an underused cut of meat, but it's so easy to cook. It's important to let it rest for about 5 minutes after taking it out of the oven to let the juices settle; otherwise your pork will be dry. Pair this with the Weeknight Garden Salad with Vinaigrette (page 90) for a complete meal.

1 (1-pound) boneless pork tenderloin

3 tablespoons extra-virgin olive oil, divided

½ teaspoon kosher salt, divided

¼ teaspoon black pepper

½ cup 2% milk

¼ cup heavy cream

1 tablespoon all-purpose flour

8 ounces white button or cremini mushrooms, thinly sliced

1. Preheat the oven to 400°F.

2. Place the pork in a medium casserole dish, drizzle with 2 tablespoons of oil, and season with ¼ teaspoon of salt and the black pepper. Rub the seasoning into the pork. Bake for 35 to 40 minutes, or until the pork's internal temperature reads 145°F on a digital thermometer. Remove the pork from the oven, cover with aluminum foil, and let rest for 5 minutes.

3. While the pork is roasting, when you have about 15 minutes left on the cooking time, mix together the milk, cream, flour, and remaining ¼ teaspoon of salt in a small bowl or measuring cup. Set aside.

4. Heat the remaining 1 tablespoon of oil in a medium skillet over medium heat, until just shimmering. Add the mushrooms and sauté for about 10 minutes, until they start to brown and there is no moisture left in the skillet.

5. Turn the heat to low, add the milk mixture, and simmer for 2 to 3 minutes, until thickened. Keep the heat on the lowest setting to keep the sauce warm until the pork is finished cooking and resting.

6. Cut the tenderloin into ¼-inch-thick slices and top with mushroom sauce. Serve.

Per serving: Calories: 295; Protein: 24g; Total carbs: 5g; Sugars: 3g; Fiber: 1g; Total fat: 20g; Saturated fat: 6g; Cholesterol: 84mg; Sodium: 332mg

CHAPTER 11

Vegetable Sides

◇◇

Cherry Tomatoes with Mozzarella and Basil Pesto

Serves 4 ♦ Prep time: 5 minutes

FEW INGREDIENTS ♦ GLUTEN-FREE ♦ UNDER 30 MINUTES ♦ VEGETARIAN

This simple side dish brings together a handful of classic flavors of Italian cuisine. It takes only five minutes, and it pairs especially well with Chicken Burger Lettuce Wraps (page 147) or Pan-Seared Tilapia with Cilantro Gremolata (page 132).

½ cup chopped walnuts

4 cups halved
cherry tomatoes

4 ounces fresh mozza-
rella cheese, cut into
½-inch cubes, or small
mozzarella balls

¼ cup basil pesto

1. Place the walnuts in a dry skillet over medium heat. Toast, shaking constantly, for 2 to 3 minutes, until they have a toasty fragrance.

2. Transfer the toasted walnuts to a medium bowl. Add the tomatoes, mozzarella cheese, and pesto, tossing together. Serve immediately.

 DID YOU KNOW? Pesto is traditionally made with basil, but it can be made with other greens, such as spinach, arugula, parsley, or even carrot tops.

Per serving: Calories: 289; Protein: 11g; Total carbs: 10g; Sugars: 2g; Fiber: 4g; Total fat: 23g; Saturated fat: 6g; Cholesterol: 24mg; Sodium: 249mg

Rosemary Balsamic Roasted Tomatoes and Red Onions

Serves 4 ◆ Prep time: 5 minutes ◆ Cook time: 15 minutes

**DAIRY-FREE ◆ FEW INGREDIENTS ◆ GLUTEN-FREE ◆ ONE PAN ◆
UNDER 30 MINUTES ◆ VEGAN**

Roasted tomatoes are the answer for off-season grocery store tomatoes, which don't have a huge flavor. Usually cherry tomatoes are good all year round, but winter makes it tough to find a tasty tomato. Luckily, roasting helps bring out the sweet flavor.

4 cups cherry tomatoes

1 small red onion, thinly sliced

1 tablespoon chopped fresh rosemary

1 tablespoon balsamic vinegar

2 tablespoons extra-virgin olive oil

¼ teaspoon kosher salt

⅛ teaspoon black pepper

1. Preheat the oven to 400°F. Line a baking sheet with aluminum foil.

2. Put the tomatoes, onion, rosemary, vinegar, oil, salt, and black pepper on the prepared baking sheet and gently toss together. Roast for 15 minutes, or until most of the tomatoes are soft.

3. Transfer to a serving dish and enjoy.

 SUBSTITUTION TIP: If you can't find cherry tomatoes, cut some regular tomatoes into pieces.

Per serving: Calories: 101; Protein: 2g; Total carbs: 8g; Sugars: 3g; Fiber: 2g; Total fat: 7g; Saturated fat: 1g; Cholesterol: 0mg; Sodium: 82mg

Parmesan Zucchini Fries

Serves 4 • Prep time: 5 minutes • Cook time: 5 minutes

FEW INGREDIENTS • GLUTEN-FREE • UNDER 30 MINUTES • VEGETARIAN

This is one of the easiest ways to get vegetables on the table in 10 minutes or less. These are a crowd pleaser in my house. I like to serve this dish with tzatziki (page 85) on the side, but you can use any healthy dipping sauce you like.

1 large (12-inch) zucchini

2 tablespoons extra-virgin olive oil

¼ teaspoon kosher salt

¼ teaspoon black pepper

½ cup freshly grated Parmesan cheese

1. Preheat the oven to broil. Line a baking sheet with aluminum foil.

2. Cut the zucchini into sticks that are about 2 inches long and ½-inch wide. Transfer them to a medium bowl. Add the oil, salt, and black pepper, tossing until the zucchini is coated.

3. Transfer the zucchini to the prepared baking sheet and sprinkle Parmesan cheese on top. Broil for 1 to 2 minutes, until the cheese just starts to melt. This will keep your zucchini fries crunchy.

4. Remove from the oven and serve immediately.

 COOKING TIP: Broilers all have different levels of intensity, depending on where you place the oven rack. Always keep a watchful eye when broiling to ensure you pull these out just when the cheese starts to melt. It doesn't take long!

Per serving: Calories: 126; Protein: 5g; Total carbs: 4g; Sugars: 2g; Fiber: 1g; Total fat: 11g; Saturated fat: 3g; Cholesterol: 11mg; Sodium: 302mg

Creamed Spinach with Parmesan

Serves 4 ✦ Prep time: 5 minutes ✦ Cook time: 10 minutes

FEW INGREDIENTS ✦ GLUTEN-FREE ✦ ONE PAN ✦ UNDER 30 MINUTES ✦ VEGETARIAN

There are so many ways to make creamed spinach. Using cream cheese is not one of the traditional ways of making this classic dish, but it adds a tanginess and creaminess that heavy cream can't give you. If you have extra cream cheese, make some Ricotta Spinach Dip (page 87).

2 tablespoons extra-virgin olive oil

1 small onion, finely chopped

1 garlic clove, minced

1 (10-ounce) package frozen spinach, thawed and liquid squeezed out

¼ cup chive cream cheese

¼ cup freshly grated Parmesan cheese

1. In a large skillet over medium heat, combine the oil and onion and sauté for about 4 minutes, until the onion is translucent.

2. Add the garlic and spinach and cook, stirring, for about 3 minutes, until heated through.

3. Add the cream cheese and Parmesan and stir for about 3 minutes, until the cream cheese has melted into the spinach. Serve.

Per serving: Calories: 155; Protein: 6g; Total carbs: 7g; Sugars: 2g; Fiber: 2g; Total fat: 12g; Saturated fat: 4g; Cholesterol: 15mg; Sodium: 241mg

Roasted Fennel with Oranges

Serves 4 ◆ Prep time: 5 minutes ◆ Cook time: 20 minutes

**DAIRY-FREE ◆ FEW INGREDIENTS ◆ GLUTEN-FREE ◆
ONE PAN ◆ UNDER 30 MINUTES ◆ VEGAN**

Fennel is an unassuming root vegetable that doesn't get the attention it deserves. It has a strong licorice flavor when raw but becomes sweeter when roasted. Pick a bulb that still has some fronds on it, which you can use for a fresh garnish.

1 (1-pound) fennel bulb

2 tablespoons extra-virgin olive oil

½ teaspoon kosher salt

2 navel oranges, peeled and sliced

Pinch black pepper

1. Preheat the oven to 425°F. Line a baking sheet with parchment paper.

2. Cut the fronds off the fennel, chop them, and reserve about 2 tablespoons for a garnish. Thinly slice the fennel bulb.

3. Transfer the fennel to the prepared baking sheet and arrange in an even layer. Drizzle with the oil and salt, tossing to coat. Roast for 20 minutes, or until the fennel is lightly browned.

4. Transfer the fennel to a serving plate and top with the oranges. Garnish with the chopped fronds and the black pepper. Serve.

Per serving: Calories: 132; Protein: 2g; Total carbs: 18g; Sugars: 11g; Fiber: 5g; Total fat: 7g; Saturated fat: 1g; Cholesterol: 0mg; Sodium: 200mg

Honey-Roasted Carrots

Serves 4 ◆ Prep time: 5 minutes ◆ Cook time: 20 minutes

**DAIRY-FREE ◆ FEW INGREDIENTS ◆ GLUTEN-FREE ◆
ONE PAN ◆ UNDER 30 MINUTES ◆ VEGETARIAN**

Roasting carrots brings out a sweetness you don't get when you eat them raw. Coupled with a light honey glaze, this healthy side dish will please even the pickiest eaters.

4 large carrots, cut into ¼-inch rounds

1½ tablespoons extra-virgin olive oil

1 tablespoon honey

¼ teaspoon kosher salt

⅛ teaspoon black pepper

¼ cup chopped fresh parsley

1. Preheat the oven to 400°F. Line a baking sheet with parchment paper.

2. Spread the carrots on the prepared baking sheet and toss with the oil, honey, salt, and black pepper. Bake for 20 minutes, or until the carrots are easily pierced with a fork.

3. Transfer the carrots to a serving bowl. Mix in the parsley and serve.

 VARIATION: Carrots are delicious roasted with a variety of spices. Try cinnamon or use some of the other spices in this book, such as turmeric, cumin, and coriander.

Per serving: Calories: 92; Protein: 1g; Total carbs: 12g; Sugars: 8g; Fiber: 2g; Total fat: 5g; Saturated fat: 1g; Cholesterol: 0mg; Sodium: 122mg

Charred Snack Peppers
with Parmesan

Serves 4 ♦ Prep time: 5 minutes ♦ Cook time: 5 minutes

FEW INGREDIENTS ♦ GLUTEN-FREE ♦ ONE PAN ♦ UNDER 30 MINUTES ♦ VEGETARIAN

Eating a Mediterranean diet for weight loss isn't just about eating raw vegetables. It's about finding a way to enjoy your favorite foods with different cooking methods and adding in extra flavors without a lot of calories. Snack peppers are great for a quick bite, but they are also delicious as a cooked side. Adding the savory flavor of Parmesan cheese elevates these seemingly simple peppers to elegant side-dish status.

1 tablespoon extra-virgin olive oil

1 (8-ounce) bag snack peppers

¼ teaspoon kosher salt

¼ cup freshly grated Parmesan cheese

2 tablespoons chopped fresh cilantro

1. In a medium skillet, heat the oil over medium heat until it shimmers. Add the peppers and cook for about 2 minutes, until they start browning on the bottom.

2. With tongs, turn each pepper and cook for another 2 minutes, until they are charred on both sides.

3. Remove from the heat and sprinkle with the salt, Parmesan cheese, and cilantro. Serve warm or at room temperature.

 DID YOU KNOW? This snack resembles the classic Spanish tapas dish *pimientos de padrón*: blistered bright green peppers that hail from the municipality of Padrón in Galicia.

Per serving: Calories: 76; Protein: 3g; Total carbs: 5g; Sugars: 2g; Fiber: 1g; Total fat: 5g; Saturated fat: 1g; Cholesterol: 5mg; Sodium: 206mg

Spicy Roasted Broccoli with Almonds

Serves 4 • Prep time: 5 minutes • Cook time: 15 minutes

DAIRY-FREE • FEW INGREDIENTS • GLUTEN-FREE • ONE PAN • UNDER 30 MINUTES • VEGAN

When you're spending time on a main dish, getting a healthy side dish on the table doesn't have to add a lot of work. Mediterranean sides are meant to be easy, wholesome, and visually appealing. This broccoli side takes mere minutes and can be timed to be ready at the same time as your main dish.

1 large head broccoli, cut into bite-size pieces (about 6 cups)

2 tablespoons extra-virgin olive oil

¼ teaspoon red pepper flakes

¼ teaspoon kosher salt

¼ teaspoon black pepper

¼ cup sliced unsalted almonds

1. Preheat the oven to 425°F. Line a baking sheet with parchment paper.

2. Spread the broccoli on the prepared baking sheet and toss with the oil, red pepper flakes, salt, and black pepper. Roast for 10 minutes, until starting to brown.

3. Remove from the oven, sprinkle the almonds on top, then return to the oven. Roast for 5 minutes, or until the almonds are toasted. Serve.

 DID YOU KNOW? You can eat the stem of your broccoli. Rather than discarding it, cut off the tough bottom tip, then cut it into pieces roughly the same size as the florets.

Per serving: Calories: 157; Protein: 6g; Total carbs: 11g; Sugars: 3g; Fiber: 5g; Total fat: 11g; Saturated fat: 1g; Cholesterol: 0mg; Sodium: 120mg

Roasted Eggplant, Zucchini, and Red Onion

Serves 4 ◆ Prep time: 5 minutes ◆ Cook time: 20 minutes

DAIRY-FREE ◆ FEW INGREDIENTS ◆ GLUTEN-FREE ◆ ONE PAN ◆ UNDER 30 MINUTES ◆ VEGAN

The secret to good roasted eggplant and zucchini is not to overcook them. This dish takes only minutes to prep, and the oven does most of the work. If you have other quick-cooking vegetables, like tomatoes or summer squash, add those for even more color.

2 tablespoons extra-virgin olive oil, divided

1 eggplant, cut into ¼-inch slices

1 zucchini, cut into ¼-inch slices

1 large red onion, cut into ¼-inch slices

½ teaspoon Italian seasoning

¼ teaspoon kosher salt

⅛ teaspoon red pepper flakes

1. Preheat the oven to 400°F. Coat a medium cast-iron skillet with 1 tablespoon of oil.

2. Arrange the vegetable slices in a ring, alternating eggplant, zucchini, and onion. Drizzle the remaining 1 tablespoon of oil over the top and sprinkle with the Italian seasoning, salt, and red pepper flakes.

3. Bake for 20 minutes, until the vegetables are soft and lightly browned on the top. Serve.

 VARIATION: A sprinkle of Parmesan or feta cheese on the top makes this a heartier side.

Per serving: Calories: 119; Protein: 2g; Total carbs: 14g; Sugars: 8g; Fiber: 5g; Total fat: 7g; Saturated fat: 1g; Cholesterol: 0mg; Sodium: 79mg

Sautéed Asparagus and Peas with Shallots and Herbs

Serves 4 ◆ Prep time: 5 minutes ◆ Cook time: 10 minutes

**DAIRY-FREE ◆ FEW INGREDIENTS ◆ GLUTEN-FREE ◆
ONE PAN ◆ UNDER 30 MINUTES ◆ VEGAN**

This super quick side dish looks amazingly elegant. My kids love peas, so I always have them in the freezer and add them to all sorts of dishes. It's an easy side to pull together when you are waiting for your main dish to finish cooking. For the fresh herbs, use what you have—dill, parsley, and basil all work well.

2 tablespoons extra-virgin olive oil

1 shallot, chopped

10 asparagus stalks, trimmed and cut into ½-inch pieces

¼ teaspoon kosher salt

2 cups thawed frozen peas

2 tablespoons minced fresh herbs of choice

1. In a medium skillet over medium heat, combine the oil, shallot, asparagus, and salt and sauté for 5 minutes, until the shallot is translucent and the asparagus is still firm.

2. Add the peas and cook for 3 to 4 minutes, or until they are warmed through.

3. Transfer to a serving bowl and toss with the herbs. Serve warm.

 VARIATION: If you don't have peas but you have a frozen mixed vegetable medley, you can use that instead.

Per serving: Calories: 123; Protein: 5g; Total carbs: 12g; Sugars: 5g; Fiber: 4g; Total fat: 7g; Saturated fat: 1g; Cholesterol: 0mg; Sodium: 144mg

Patatas Bravas with Paprika Yogurt

Serves 4 ✦ Prep time: 5 minutes ✦ Cook time: 25 minutes

FEW INGREDIENTS ✦ GLUTEN-FREE ✦ VEGETARIAN

On my family's second trip to Spain, we stopped to get tapas as soon as we arrived. I had to get patatas bravas. These little potato bites are usually deep-fried and served with a flavored spicy mayonnaise drizzle. I've lightened it up and made it heart-healthy by roasting the potatoes and adding a yogurt sauce instead of mayo.

3 cups cubed Yukon Gold or red potatoes

2 tablespoons canola oil

½ teaspoon kosher salt

¼ cup plain full-fat Greek yogurt

½ teaspoon paprika

1. Preheat the oven to 450°F. Line a baking sheet with parchment paper.

2. Place the potatoes in a medium bowl. Add the oil and salt, tossing to combine. Transfer the potatoes to the prepared baking sheet and arrange them in an even layer.

3. Roast for 25 minutes, or until the potatoes are golden brown.

4. While the potatoes are roasting, mix together the yogurt and paprika in a small bowl.

5. Serve the potatoes hot with dollops of yogurt on top.

 COOKING TIP: It's best to use a neutral oil with a high smoking point, like canola, when cooking at very high temperatures. While canola oil gets a bad rap, in moderation it is a good source of heart-healthy monounsaturated fat—as long as it is labeled "expeller pressed," which means no chemicals were used to extract it.

Per serving: Calories: 154; Protein: 3g; Total carbs: 21g; Sugars: 2g; Fiber: 2g; Total fat: 8g; Saturated fat: 1g; Cholesterol: 2mg; Sodium: 181mg

Parmesan Baked Potatoes

Serves 4 ◆ Prep time: 10 minutes ◆ Cook time: 30 minutes

FEW INGREDIENTS ◆ GLUTEN-FREE ◆ ONE PAN ◆ VEGETARIAN

Potatoes are wrongly considered off-limits on a weight-loss diet because of their association with fried fast foods. But when cooked in a healthy way and eaten in moderation, they can and should be enjoyed with pleasure and without guilt. A popular vegetable around the Mediterranean, they are a delicious source of potassium, vitamin C, and fiber.

2 tablespoons extra-virgin olive oil, divided

1 garlic clove, peeled and grated

4 Yukon Gold or russet potatoes, very thinly sliced (about 1 pound)

½ cup freshly grated Parmesan cheese, divided

½ teaspoon kosher salt, divided

1. Preheat the oven to 425°F.

2. In a 6-inch or 8-inch casserole dish, brush 1 tablespoon of oil along the bottom and sides of the dish. Spread out the garlic on the bottom.

3. Put down one layer of potatoes and sprinkle 2 tablespoons of Parmesan cheese and ⅛ teaspoon of salt. Repeat for three more layers. Drizzle the remaining 1 tablespoon of oil over the top.

4. Roast for 30 minutes, or until a fork easily pierces the potatoes. Serve.

 DID YOU KNOW? With its strong and sharp taste, Parmesan cheese is great on a weight-loss diet because a little goes a long way. It's also a low-lactose cheese that's high in calcium and phosphorus, which promotes bone health.

Per serving: Calories: 192; Protein: 6g; Total carbs: 21g; Sugars: 1g; Fiber: 2g; Total fat: 10g; Saturated fat: 3g; Cholesterol: 11mg; Sodium: 366mg

CHAPTER 12

Sweets

Easy Mango Ice Cream

Serves 4 • Prep time: 5 minutes

FEW INGREDIENTS • GLUTEN-FREE • UNDER 30 MINUTES • VEGETARIAN

This is a popular recipe in my house. My children are very creative with the blender and experiment with using different frozen fruits with milk—which led to the discovery of this delicious frozen treat that has none of the added sugar of regular ice cream.

2 cups frozen mango pieces

½ cup 2% milk

Place the mango and milk in a blender and blend for 2 to 3 minutes, until it is smooth and creamy, scraping down the sides as needed. Serve.

 COOKING TIP: Even if you're cooking for one, make a full recipe of this and keep the extra in the freezer. Just let it thaw on the counter for at least 5 minutes before eating to soften it up.

Per serving: Calories: 60; Protein: 2g; Total carbs: 12g; Sugars: 11g; Fiber: 1g; Total fat: 1g; Saturated fat: <1g; Cholesterol: 2mg; Sodium: 14mg

Lemon Granita

Serves 4 ◆ Prep time: 5 minutes, plus 2 hours to chill ◆ Cook time: 1 minute

DAIRY-FREE ◆ FEW INGREDIENTS ◆ GLUTEN-FREE ◆ VEGAN

Lemons are abundant in Italy. On a trip to Naples, I noticed them in the popular local liqueur limoncello and in eateries selling handmade lemon granita. A semifrozen sorbet-like dessert, granita originally hails from the southern island of Sicily. This recipe captures the zesty flavor of Italy's favorite citrus in a classic dessert.

1½ cups water

⅓ cup sugar

Zest and juice of 2 lemons

1. In a small saucepan over medium heat, bring the water to a simmer. Add the sugar and wait 1 minute for the sugar to dissolve.

2. Add the lemon zest and juice and stir well to combine. Transfer the lemon mixture into a shallow freezer-safe container and freeze for 1 hour.

3. Take it out of the freezer and scrape it with a sturdy fork. It will be slushy.

4. Freeze again for 45 to 60 minutes, or until the granita on the outside edges is frozen again and the inside is still slushy. Scrape again with a fork before serving.

 VARIATION: You can use the same formula of water and sugar and vary this recipe by using ½ cup of any citrus juice instead of lemon juice, such as orange or lime, with their zest.

Per serving: Calories: 71; Protein: <1g; Total carbs: 19g; Sugars: 17g; Fiber: <1g; Total fat: <1g; Saturated fat: 0g; Cholesterol: 0mg; Sodium: 1mg

Strawberry Frozen Yogurt Drops

Serves 2 ◆ Prep time: 10 minutes, plus 2 hours to chill

FEW INGREDIENTS ◆ GLUTEN-FREE ◆ VEGETARIAN

This recipe was inspired by my 12-year-old daughter. I don't like to keep ice cream in the freezer all the time, and in need of a sweet treat, she concocted these yogurt drops with what was on hand. She just wanted something cold and sweet, which is exactly what this dessert gives you.

1 cup plain full-fat
Greek yogurt

2 tablespoons
strawberry jam

2 teaspoons honey

1. Line a small baking sheet or freezer-safe plate with parchment paper.

2. In a small bowl, mix together the yogurt, jam, and honey.

3. Transfer the mixture to a small zip-top bag and cut off one of the bottom corners—just enough to squeeze out a small amount of the mixture. Squeeze out ¼-inch drops onto the parchment paper.

4. Place the drops in the freezer to chill for at least 2 hours.

5. After the drops are frozen, eat them immediately, or transfer them to an airtight container and store them in the freezer for snacking.

 COOKING TIP: This is a great recipe to use up any Greek yogurt and strawberry jam you may have in the refrigerator.

Per serving: Calories: 175; Protein: 11g; Total carbs: 23g; Sugars: 22g; Fiber: 0g; Total fat: 5g; Saturated fat: 3g; Cholesterol: 19mg; Sodium: 46mg

Whipped Ricotta with Cherries, Honey, and Pistachios

Serves 4 ◆ Prep time: 10 minutes

FEW INGREDIENTS ◆ GLUTEN-FREE ◆ UNDER 30 MINUTES ◆ VEGETARIAN

Whipped ricotta makes a wonderfully fluffy dessert when paired with berries, nuts, and a drizzle of honey. Ricotta is the Italian version of cottage cheese, and most of the time they can be used interchangeably. Both are high in protein and great for a weight-loss plan, especially when you buy low-fat versions. If you have leftover ricotta from the Crostini and Berry Plate with Feta-Ricotta Spread (page 63) or Ricotta Spinach Dip with Carrot Sticks (page 87), this is the perfect way to use it up.

1⅓ cups part-skim ricotta cheese

2 cups fresh or thawed frozen pitted unsweetened cherries

4 teaspoons honey

4 tablespoons chopped unsalted pistachios

1. Place the ricotta cheese in a small bowl. Using an electric hand mixer, whip it for 3 to 4 minutes, until it's light and fluffy.

2. Divide the cheese among four serving bowls and top each with ½ cup of cherries, 1 teaspoon of honey, and 1 tablespoon of pistachios. Serve.

 COOKING TIP: If you don't have a hand mixer, use a whisk to whip the ricotta. It just takes a few minutes longer.

Per serving: Calories: 222; Protein: 12g; Total carbs: 23g; Sugars: 16g; Fiber: 2g; Total fat: 10g; Saturated fat: 5g; Cholesterol: 25mg; Sodium: 82mg

Vanilla Baked Pears

Serves 4 • Prep time: 5 minutes • Cook time: 20 minutes

**DAIRY-FREE • FEW INGREDIENTS • GLUTEN-FREE • ONE PAN •
UNDER 30 MINUTES • VEGAN**

I am a firm believer in fruit for dessert, but you don't have to simply put fruit in a bowl. If you love a fruit crisp, you're going to love this dessert. Use any nuts you want in this, but walnuts are great as a plant-based source of omega-3 fatty acids. Use extra walnuts in the Fruit and Honey Yogurt Parfait (page 61).

4 ripe pears

½ cup gluten-free
  old-fashioned rolled oats

¼ cup chopped walnuts

1 teaspoon vanilla extract

2 tablespoons light or dark
  brown sugar

1. Preheat the oven to 400°F. Line a baking sheet with aluminum foil.

2. Halve the pears lengthwise and spoon out the core, making a hole for the filling.

3. Place the oats, walnuts, vanilla, and brown sugar in a blender or food processor and pulse until well blended. Stuff each pear with the oat mixture and place them on the prepared baking sheet.

4. Bake for 20 minutes, or until the oat mixture is golden brown on top. Serve.

 COOKING TIP: If your pears are rocking around too much on the pan and spilling the filling, cut a small slice off the rounded back so they sit flat on the baking sheet.

Per serving: Calories: 207; Protein: 3g; Total carbs: 39g; Sugars: 22g; Fiber: 7g; Total fat: 6g; Saturated fat: 1g; Cholesterol: 0mg; Sodium: 3mg

Orange and Honey Polenta Bars

Makes 9 bars • Prep time: 15 minutes • Cook time: 20 minutes

DAIRY-FREE • GLUTEN-FREE • VEGETARIAN

This recipe draws its inspiration from polenta cake. While it's a dessert that typically contains a lot of butter and the associated saturated fat, these bars use heart-healthy olive oil instead to produce a moist and luscious treat, naturally sweetened with orange zest and honey. Store these bars in an airtight container on the counter for up to two days, then transfer to the refrigerator for up to three days more.

Nonstick cooking spray

1 cup polenta

1 cup almond flour

1 teaspoon baking powder

¼ teaspoon table salt

½ cup extra-virgin olive oil

¼ cup honey

2 large eggs

1 teaspoon vanilla extract

Zest of 1 large orange

2 tablespoons powdered sugar (optional)

1. Preheat the oven to 350°F. Spray an 8-by-8-inch baking dish with nonstick cooking spray.

2. In a medium bowl, mix together the polenta, almond flour, baking powder, and salt. Make a well in the middle of the dry ingredients and add the oil, honey, eggs, vanilla, and orange zest. Stir together until everything is fully combined.

3. Pour the cake batter into the prepared baking dish and bake for 20 minutes, or until a toothpick inserted into the center comes out clean.

4. Let cake cool completely in the pan, then dust with the powdered sugar (if using). Cut into 9 bars and serve.

❖ **COOKING TIP:** Since this recipe uses only the zest, keep that orange in the refrigerator to juice in the morning.

Per serving (1 bar): Calories: 281; Protein: 5g; Total carbs: 23g; Sugars: 9g; Fiber: 2g; Total fat: 20g; Saturated fat: 3g; Cholesterol: 37mg; Sodium: 134mg

Chocolate Almond Oat Cookies

Makes 20 cookies ◆ Prep time: 15 minutes ◆ Cook time: 10 minutes

DAIRY-FREE ◆ GLUTEN-FREE ◆ UNDER 30 MINUTES ◆ VEGETARIAN

Eating a plant-forward diet doesn't mean you can't enjoy dessert. These cookies are the perfect treat with plant-based ingredients that will soon become staples in your pantry. These cookies will keep for two days in an airtight container on the counter, or you can keep them in the refrigerator for five days.

¼ cup canola oil

¼ cup honey

½ teaspoon vanilla extract

1 large egg

⅛ teaspoon table salt

1 cup almond flour

½ cup gluten-free
   old-fashioned rolled oats

2 tablespoons unsweetened
   cocoa powder

½ teaspoon baking powder

1. Preheat the oven to 350°F. Line two baking sheets with parchment paper.

2. In a medium bowl, stir together the oil, honey, vanilla, egg, and salt. Add the almond flour, oats, cocoa powder, and baking powder and stir until combined.

3. Using a 1-tablespoon measure, scoop balls of dough onto the prepared baking sheets, leaving 2 inches between each one. You should have about 10 cookies per sheet.

4. Bake for 10 minutes, or until a toothpick inserted into one cookie comes out clean.

5. Cool completely on a cooling rack, then serve.

 COOKING TIP: Leave plenty of space between these cookies for them to spread out as they bake. You should end up with about 20; bake them in two batches if needed.

Per serving (2 cookies): Calories: 164; Protein: 4g; Total carbs: 13g; Sugars: 8g; Fiber: 2g; Total fat: 12g; Saturated fat: 1g; Cholesterol: 19mg; Sodium: 48mg

Bananas Foster Crepes with Whipped Cream

Serves 4 ◆ Prep time: 10 minutes, plus 30 minutes to chill ◆ Cook time: 10 minutes

VEGETARIAN

I have a bit of a love affair with crepes. They are a staple at European Christmas markets and invoke a warm, comforting feeling when we make them at home. This recipe cuts out unnecessary sugar in the crepe itself and instead adds it to the bananas to make a rich glaze.

1 cup all-purpose flour

2 large eggs

1¼ cups 2% milk

1 teaspoon vanilla extract

⅛ teaspoon kosher salt

Nonstick cooking spray

1½ tablespoons unsalted butter

2 tablespoons light or dark brown sugar

2 large bananas, cut into ¼-inch slices

½ cup heavy cream

1. To make the crepe batter, place the flour, eggs, milk, vanilla, and salt in a blender and blend until smooth. Let this mixture chill in the refrigerator for 30 minutes or up to 2 hours.

2. Spray a small nonstick skillet with nonstick cooking spray and set it over medium-low heat. Add ¼ cup of the crepe batter to the pan. Swirl the batter around the pan until it forms a complete circle. Cook for about 30 seconds, until you can easily slide a spatula underneath, then carefully flip the crepe over and cook for about 20 seconds, or until the bottom is lightly browned. Repeat until all the crepes are cooked.

3. In the same skillet over medium-low heat, add the butter and brown sugar and stir for about 1 minute, until they're combined and melted. Add the bananas, stir to coat, and remove from the heat.

4. Add the cream to a medium bowl and whip on high with an electric hand mixer for 4 to 5 minutes, or until stiff peaks form.

5. Add 4 to 5 banana slices to each crepe, roll it up, and top with whipped cream. Serve.

 DID YOU KNOW? While crepes are especially popular in France, this recipe is inspired by the food of New Orleans, where there is a long history of fusing French and Southern cuisine.

Per serving: Calories: 406; Protein: 10g; Total carbs: 49g; Sugars: 18g; Fiber: 3g; Total fat: 19g; Saturated fat: 11g; Cholesterol: 133mg; Sodium: 109mg

Measurement Conversions

VOLUME EQUIVALENTS (LIQUID)

US Standard	US Standard (ounces)	Metric (approximate)
2 tablespoons	1 fl. oz.	30 mL
¼ cup	2 fl. oz.	60 mL
½ cup	4 fl. oz.	120 mL
1 cup	8 fl. oz.	240 mL
1½ cups	12 fl. oz.	355 mL
2 cups or 1 pint	16 fl. oz.	475 mL
4 cups or 1 quart	32 fl. oz.	1 L
1 gallon	128 fl. oz.	4 L

OVEN TEMPERATURES

Fahrenheit (F)	Celsius (C) (approximate)
250°F	120°C
300°F	150°C
325°F	165°C
350°F	180°C
375°F	190°C
400°F	200°C
425°F	220°C
450°F	230°C

VOLUME EQUIVALENTS (DRY)

US Standard	Metric (approximate)
⅛ teaspoon	0.5 mL
¼ teaspoon	1 mL
½ teaspoon	2 mL
¾ teaspoon	4 mL
1 teaspoon	5 mL
1 tablespoon	15 mL
¼ cup	59 mL
⅓ cup	79 mL
½ cup	118 mL
⅔ cup	156 mL
¾ cup	177 mL
1 cup	235 mL
2 cups or 1 pint	475 mL
3 cups	700 mL
4 cups or 1 quart	1 L

WEIGHT EQUIVALENTS

US Standard	Metric (approximate)
½ ounce	15 g
1 ounce	30 g
2 ounces	60 g
4 ounces	115 g
8 ounces	225 g
12 ounces	340 g
16 ounces or 1 pound	455 g

References

Donnelly, Joseph E., Steven N. Blair, John M. Jakicic, Melinda M. Manore, Janet W. Rankin, Bryan K. Smith, and American College of Sports Medicine. "American College of Sports Medicine Position Stand: Appropriate Physical Activity Intervention Strategies for Weight Loss and Prevention of Weight Regain for Adults." *Medicine and Science in Sports and Exercise* 41, no. 2 (2009): 459–471. doi:10.1249/MSS.0b013e3181949333.

Echouffo-Tcheugui, Justin B., and Rexford S. Ahima. "Does Diet Quality or Nutrient Quantity Contribute More to Health?" *The Journal of Clinical Investigation* 129, no. 10 (2019): 3969–3970. doi:10.1172/JCI131449.

Ferrer-Cascales, Rosario, Natalia Albaladejo-Blázquez, Nicolás Ruiz-Robledillo, Violeta Clement-Carbonell, Miriam Sánchez-San Segundo, and Ana Zaragoza-Martí. "Higher Adherence to the Mediterranean Diet Is Related to More Subjective Happiness in Adolescents: The Role of Health-Related Quality of Life." *Nutrients* 11, no. 3 (2019): 698. doi:10.3390/nu11030698.

Huang, Qingyi, Huan Liu, Katsuhiko Suzuki, Sihui Ma, and Chunhong Liu. "Linking What We Eat to Our Mood: A Review of Diet, Dietary Antioxidants, and Depression." *Antioxidants* 8, no. 9 (2019): 376. doi:10.3390/antiox8090376.

Knox, Emily, and Jose Joaquin Muros. "Association of Lifestyle Behaviours with Self-Esteem through Health-Related Quality of Life in Spanish Adolescents." *European Journal of Pediatrics* 176, no. 5 (2017): 621–628. doi:10.1007/s00431-017-2886-z.

Koliaki, Chrysi, Theodoros Spinos, Marianna Spinou, Maria-Eugenia Brinia, Dimitra Mitsopoulou, and Nicholas Katsilambros. "Defining the Optimal Dietary Approach for Safe, Effective and Sustainable Weight Loss in Overweight and Obese Adults." *Healthcare* 6, no. 3 (2018): 73. doi:10.3390/healthcare6030073.

Lăcătușu, Cristina-Mihaela, Elena-Daniela Grigorescu, Mariana Floria, Alina Onofriescu, and Bogdan-Mircea Mihai. "The Mediterranean Diet: From an Environment-Driven Food Culture to an Emerging Medical Prescription." *International Journal of Environmental Research and Public Health* 16, no. 6 (2019): 942. doi:10.3390/ijerph16060942.

Miketinas, Derek, George A. Bray, Robbie A. Beyl, Donna H. Ryan, Frank M. Sacks, and Catherine M. Champagne. "Fiber Intake Predicts Weight Loss and Dietary Adherence in Adults Consuming Calorie-Restricted Diets: The POUNDS Lost (Preventing Overweight Using Novel Dietary Strategies) Study." *The Journal of Nutrition* 149, no. 10 (2019): 1742–1748. doi:10.1093/jn/nxz117.

National Institute of Diabetes and Digestive and Kidney Diseases. "Body Weight Planner." NIDDK.NIH.gov/bwp.

National Institutes of Health. "Sleep Deprivation and Deficiency." NHLBI.NIH.gov /health-topics/sleep-deprivation-and-deficiency.

Skarupski, Kimberly A., C. C. Tangney, H. Li, D. A. Evans, and M. C. Morris. "Mediterranean Diet and Depressive Symptoms among Older Adults over Time." *The Journal of Nutrition, Health, and Aging* 17, no. 5 (2013): 441–445. doi:10.1007 /s12603-012-0437-x.

Smethers, Alissa D., and Barbara J. Rolls. "Dietary Management of Obesity: Cornerstones of Healthy Eating Patterns." *The Medical Clinics of North America* 102, no. 1 (2018): 107–124. doi:10.1016/j.mcna.2017.08.009.

U.S. Department of Health and Human Services. "Dietary Guidelines for Americans 2015–2020." Health.gov/our-work/food-nutrition/2015-2020-dietary-guidelines.

van der Valk, Eline S., Mesut Savas, and Elisabeth F. C. van Rossum. "Stress and Obesity: Are There More Susceptible Individuals?" *Current Obesity Reports* 7, no. 2 (2018): 193–203. doi:10.1007/s13679-018-0306-y.

Whalen, Kristine A., Marjorie L. McCullough, W. Dana Flanders, Terryl J. Hartman, Suzanne Judd, and Roberd M. Bostick. "Paleolithic and Mediterranean Diet Pattern Scores Are Inversely Associated with Biomarkers of Inflammation and Oxidative Balance in Adults." *The Journal of Nutrition* 146, no. 6 (2016): 1217–1226. doi:10.3945 /jn.115.224048.

Index

Acknowledgments

The evolution of a cookbook does not happen with the quickness of a chop or the click of a mouse. It takes months of dedicated hands and minds of the best people. And I have had the best.

I want to first thank my family. Writing a cookbook is a family affair, and we were all in. They analyzed every recipe—what they liked, what didn't work, and what could be changed. They critiqued with grace and purpose, because they know the importance of a solid recipe.

To my amazing recipe testers: There are too many to name, but I can't thank you enough for your honest and helpful feedback. I couldn't have written these recipes without you. This book also belongs to you.

To my fellow dietitians: I see you spreading the word that food heals, nourishes, and brings joy. Your dedication to our profession is inspiring. Keep up the good fight and continue to teach that good nutrition means good health. Serena Ball, thank you for your guidance on this book, your support, and the friendship you have blessed me with. I will always cherish it.

To all of my friends over the years: my Air Force friends, my military spouse friends, my high school and college friends, my old friends and new friends. Your support in all of my endeavors has never gone unnoticed. You always answer the call and are the best village I could ask for.

Thank you to Callisto Media for taking a chance on me and my love for cooking and health. This book has been an absolute pleasure from start to finish. Thank you to Adrian Potts. Your editing makes me look good and your encouragement through every step of the process helped me grow as a writer and recipe developer.

The most important shout-out goes to my husband, who desperately loves leftovers but went without them for months while I tested four-serving recipes for our family of five. Thank you for your patience.

About the Author

Sarah Pflugradt, MS, RDN, CSCS, is the voice behind Sarah Pflugradt Nutrition (SarahPflugradt .com), a website to promote healthy eating for active families. Her focus is to provide research-backed advice for parents of kids in sports to help them grow and excel through good nutrition. Her love of Mediterranean cooking comes from an extensive amount of time living and traveling throughout Europe.

Sarah has been a registered dietitian and nutrition expert for 10 years, working in clinical care, outpatient weight management, WIC, and private practice, and she has been an adjunct professor for Southwestern Illinois College and Park University. She is also a freelance writer and is working toward her PhD in health and human performance at Concordia University, Chicago.

Sarah currently lives in southwest Germany with her husband and three children. She accepts the challenge of cooking in her tiny German kitchen and calls it a win that her American-size baking sheet fits in her little oven.

CPSIA information can be obtained
at www.ICGtesting.com
Printed in the USA
JSHW010034250621
16143JS00002B/2